THE LITTLE RED GUARD

"A gripping, lyrical memoir . . . Revealing, ironic, and effortlessly elegant, Huang's book unpacks the paradox of China through a story about an unusual, and proverbial, Chinese box—a coffin. Just as the hazardous journey of Addie Bundren's casket on muddy country roads maps a fantastic Faulknerian world by the Mississippi, the long march of Grandma's shou mu, floating down the river of Huang's memory and imagination, projects a kaleidoscopic vista of contemporary China and paints a tortured smile of Chinese humanity."

—*Chicago Tribune*

"Delightful . . . A book that brings a corner of modern China alive—a book filled with humor, family squabbles, and ordinary life in a large city in a one-party state . . . [With] echoes of J. D. Salinger."

—*The Wall Street Journal*

"There is no overstating the profound effect of the Cultural Revolution on the lives of every single Chinese, and the Huang family's struggles to bury their grandma is a heartrending example . . . Perfect, moving."

—*The Daily Beast*

"A memoir centered on a coffin? Yes, and it works."

—*O, The Oprah Magazine*

"An interesting look at China through the lens of family."

—*New York Post*

"Mesmerizing and lyrical."

—*The (Newark) Star-Ledger*

"A riveting, well-crafted story . . . At times comic and at times heartbreaking . . . There are plenty of fresh and unforgettable revelations."
                                                                                    —Oprah.com

"Illuminating . . . Huang's coming-of-age story eloquently describes his family coping with change and how, in a turbulent time, he made sense of the world."
                                                                 —*Publishers Weekly* (starred review)

"A trenchantly observed story that depicts the clash of traditional and modern Chinese culture with a powerful combination of sensitivity and mordant irony."
                                                                                    —*Kirkus Reviews*

"[Huang's] description of life under Mao will come as a revelation to readers."
                                                                                    —*Booklist*

"Another interesting way to look at China, something readers crave."
                                                                                    —*Library Journal*

"*The Little Red Guard* is a remarkable memoir. Wenguang Huang gave it an ingenious dramatic structure, which reveals the tensions and emotional struggles within his family. At the psychological level, the story has universal resonance that is beyond history and culture. Huang tells it with extraordinary candor, acuity, and the cruel irony of life. As a result, the story is full of gravity, absurdity, and grief."
                                                                  —Ha Jin, author of *Waiting*

"*The Little Red Guard*—his first book—establishes Wenguang Huang as a master storyteller. Vividly engaging and often surprising, this memoir of coming of age in an ordinary Chinese family amid the social and political wreckage of Mao's Cultural Revolution is uncommonly wise and deeply moving."
          —Philip Gourevitch, author of *The Ballad of Abu Ghraib* and *We Wish
          to Inform You That Tomorrow We Will Be Killed with Our Families*

THE
LITTLE
RED
GUARD

a family memoir

WENGUANG HUANG

RIVERHEAD BOOKS

New York

RIVERHEAD BOOKS
Published by the Penguin Group
Penguin Group (USA) Inc.
375 Hudson Street, New York, New York 10014, USA

USA / Canada / UK / Ireland / Australia / New Zealand / India / South Africa / China

Penguin Books Ltd., Registered Offices: 80 Strand, London WC2R 0RL, England
For more information about the Penguin Group, visit penguin.com

Riverhead trade paperback ISBN: 978-1-59448-655-5

The Library of Congress has catalogued the Riverhead hardcover edition as follows:

Huang, Wenguang.
The little red guard: a family memoir / Wenguang Huang.
p.   cm.
ISBN 978-1-59448-829-0
1. Huang, Wenguang, 1964— Family.   2. Xi'an Shi (China)—Biography.
3. Huang family.   4. China—Social life and customs—1949–1976.   I. Title.
DS797.68.X536H83   2012   2011049342
929.20951—dc23

First Riverhead hardcover edition: April 2012
First Riverhead trade paperback edition: April 2013

PRINTED IN THE UNITED STATES OF AMERICA

10   9   8   7   6   5   4   3   2

Cover design by Keith Hayes
Cover photograph © Manuel Litran / Corbis
Book design by Chris Welch

While the author has made every effort to provide accurate telephone numbers and Internet addresses
at the time of publication, neither the author nor the publisher is responsible for errors, or for changes
that occur after publication. Further, the publisher does not have any control over and does not
assume any responsibility for author or third-party websites or their content.

Penguin is committed to publishing works of quality and integrity.
In that spirit, we are proud to offer this book to our readers;
however the story, the experiences, and the words
are the author's alone.

For my father

PART ONE

1.

DEMANDS

At the age of ten, I slept next to a coffin that Father had made for Grandma's seventy-third birthday. He forbade us from calling it a "coffin" and insisted that we refer to it as *shou mu*, which means something like "longevity wood." To me, it seemed a strange name for the box in which we'd bury Grandma, but it served a practical purpose. It was less spooky to share my room with a "longevity wood" than with a big black coffin.

In 1973, Grandma had turned seventy-one, or seventy-two by the Chinese counting in which you are already one at birth. All of a sudden, she became obsessed with death and was scared. My sister, Wenxia, and I still remember the night when Grandma first broached the topic. Over dinner, Mother had launched into her usual tirade over household chores. She had visited a neighbor's house the night before and seen how their eldest son willingly pitched in to wash dishes after dinner. "He polished the stove squeaky clean," Mother said, looking at the four of us. "Too bad I have given birth to a bunch of lazybones." We all hunched over our bowls silently. Grandma, impatient with Mother's whining about mundane household tasks, announced that she might die soon.

It never occurred to us children that Grandma would die someday. Ever since I could remember, she had seemed old, with wrinkles and brownish age spots on her face.

Father put down his chopsticks, looking startled and concerned. "Are you feeling sick?"

"Not . . . yet."

Mother couldn't resist. "What do you mean by that?"

It turned out her fear was based on the old Chinese adage, "When a person reaches the ages of seventy-three or eighty-four, the King of Hell is most likely to make his call." Considering that she had only one year to reach that first threshold, Grandma wanted to be ready. She asked Father to start planning her funeral. Following her death, Grandma wanted to be buried in her native village in Henan Province, next to my late grandpa.

Annoyed that she had been upstaged by Grandma, Mother left the table. Father looked relieved that his mother wasn't suffering from some serious physical ailment. "Don't start imagining things," he said. "It's a new society now and people no longer believe in those superstitious sayings." He picked up his chopsticks and went back to slurping his noodles.

Grandma never went to school, but she had a library full of sayings in her head and dispensed them freely. A few months before, a neighbor was planning a small banquet at home to celebrate her father's upcoming fiftieth birthday. She came to Grandma to seek advice on a proper gift for her father, but ended up getting an earful on why she should give up on the plan. "Back in our village, people never celebrated their birthdays before they turned sixty," she said, and backed up her point with a Chinese saying, "Enjoying a banquet of meat and drink at sixty, one's life would never cease." Grandma warned that making a fuss over one's birthdays too early could harm longevity. Our young neighbor nodded gratefully.

When I heard the story, I asked Grandma to explain the science behind it. She brushed me off. "If it has been passed down from generation to generation, it has to be true," she told me. In later years, I was surprised to hear friends who grew up in different parts of the country repeat a similar saying about celebrating birthdays at sixty, echoing what Grandma had said to our young neighbor.

We thought Grandma's new obsession with death was a phase and she would snap out of it soon, but as the cold, dark winter approached, she began to sleep less and less and the subject seemed to linger on the edge of every conversation. Oftentimes, Grandma would pretend to chat with me and my siblings at dinner, but we all knew she meant for my parents, especially Father, to hear. She said people in her native village were very particular about burials—the location and maintenance of *yin-zhai*, or residences of the dead, were believed to be critical to the well-being of the future generations. In addition, people spent extravagantly on funerals because it was considered an ultimate expression of filial duty. Grandma then recounted the story of a virtuous young woman in a poor family near her village, kneeling on the street and offering to sell her body so she could collect money to give her deceased father a proper burial.

According to Grandma, the Huang family clan had a harmonious and prosperous life in a village in the northwest of Henan Province, on the northern bank of the Yellow River. In the late 1920s, tuberculosis hit the village and Grandpa was one of the first to succumb. It was a bloody death. The family paid a well-known feng shui master who recommended moving the family cemetery plot outside the village, next to the Yellow River, as a way to stem the outbreak. In those days, there was a popular legend about a big dragon resting under the Yellow River at the very point where it bordered Grandma's village. The feng shui master assured everyone that the spot he had chosen for Grandpa straddled the dragon's back. "The new burial ground will bring luck to our family," Grandma continued. "When I reunite with Grandpa in my next life, a generation cycle will be complete. It's good for all of you."

Grandma repeated the story countless times. We would look at one another and mouth her words as she spoke them. My elder sister would call Grandma a superstitious woman. Even Father agreed and told Grandma not to tell the story again.

At first, my parents ignored Grandma's plea, but she only became more determined. During a chat with a neighbor, she learned a startling fact—burial had been outlawed in our city of Xi'an. The neighbor said that if a city dweller died in the hospital, the doctor wouldn't allow relatives to take the body home. It went to a big icebox in the morgue and then was sent for cremation. A young man had bribed the morgue keeper and retrieved his mother's body so he could have it buried. He was caught, and the police intercepted the corpse and sent it straight to the crematorium, so he had no time to perform even perfunctory rituals.

Grandma was in a panic. She seldom left our residential complex and was clueless about the changes sweeping China. She got most of her news from neighbors, from my parents and from me. Sometimes, knowing the kind of stories she liked to hear, I would make one up to get her attention, but I didn't dare lie when Grandma asked me about the cremation law. Yet in telling the truth, I scared her. She waited until Mother was outside chatting with her friends and approached Father, who was sipping tea by a coal-burning stove near the front door. She sat down on a chair next to him, had me bring her a basin of hot water so she could soak her tiny bound feet. "Jiu-er," she said, using Father's pet name. "Please don't burn me after I die. Will you promise me that?"

My sister and I were doing our homework under the light of the single bulb that lit the room. The word "burn" caught my attention. I watched Grandma and Father from the corner of my eye.

"I've told you, there is nothing to be afraid of," Father said, sounding a little impatient. "What difference does it make? When we die, our mind and body cease to exist. You won't know or feel anything."

Grandma shook her head; her face was a grimace of horror. "No . . . I don't want to be *tortured* in fire after I die," she said. How would she reunite with her husband in the next life if her body was reduced to ashes? As they talked, Grandma grew more and more agitated, and began stomping her tiny feet, sending the water from the basin splashing across the floor.

Father stood up and grabbed a towel for her to dry her feet and spoke softly, "We'll talk later. Let's not interrupt your grandchildren's homework."

Father found himself in a difficult situation. Initially, he fully intended to follow the regulations—bring Grandma's ashes home, hold a simple ceremony, and then bury the urn next to Grandpa. The practice of burial had been banned since the Communist takeover in 1949 and the government stepped up its crackdown in the mid-1970s. The mandate for cremation carried both practical and ideological reasons—burial wasted land that might otherwise be used for agriculture or buildings. Land for farming was scarce; urban residents were crammed into smaller and smaller dingy apartments. Father saw sense in the policy and tried to reason with Grandma. In the 1960s and 1970s, China faced threats from the Soviet Union and the United States, which then had a heavy military presence in Southeast Asia. To protect China's industry from possible attack by "Soviet Revisionists" and "American Imperialists," the government moved many strategic industries inland. Xi'an was chosen for the manufacture of military equipment and heavy machinery and as the site of universities and scientific research institutions. Within a few years, the city's population exploded to six million (now eight million). As a result, Father said many young people at his company couldn't get married because there was nowhere for them to live. They waited years to be assigned an apartment. In other words, the dead had to make room for the living. And traditional funeral rituals were expensive, and rife with Buddhist and Taoist tradition, which was contrary to Communist ideology.

At the time, the Cultural Revolution, though winding down, had not yet run its course. Chairman Mao's political campaigns in the early 1970s included condemnation of Confucius and the eradication of old traditions and rituals. Funerals and weddings were simplified to reflect these views. Father said he had attended a public denunciation against a company official who gave his son a traditional wedding ceremony. Someone from the village with a grudge against the official tipped off the authorities that he had hired a red sedan chair to carry the bride and paid a band to play traditional operatic tunes. The official's denunciation was severe. Walls were plastered with big white posters painted with black characters: TRANSFORM OLD TRADITIONS AND CUSTOMS! LIVE SIMPLY AND OPPOSE WASTE! Posters even covered an outside wall of the communal lavatory in our residential complex.

For me, the thought of dumping Grandma's body into a furnace was rather scary, but at school we were taught that the traditional burial was a symbol of the decadent and cruel past of the pre-Communist era. There was a popular picture book for schoolchildren, *A Silver Dollar*, which told of a poor family in Father's home province of Henan. During the famine of 1942, the family sold the daughter to a wealthy landlord as a maid. When his mother died, the landlord killed the girl by putting mercury in her drink so that she could serve his mother in the afterworld. At the funeral procession, pallbearers carried the girl sitting on a seat in the lotus position, with a fake lamp in her hands. The mercury preserved her peachy skin color, making her look as if she were alive. The story horrified me, making me believe traditional funerals to be abhorrent.

Superstition, I thought, was worthy of condemnation. At school, I was the head of the "Little Red Guards." During the annual singing contest, my classmates and I performed a song called "Down with Confucius, Oppose Old Rituals." I even helped put together a display on the school bulletin board that featured a cartoon of a big "revolutionary" fist pounding on an old man who was supposed to be Confucius. Grandma would hear nothing of my political activities at school. She even said Confucius was a saint. I was often vexed by her adherence to the old ways. On most things, I could bring her around with Father's help, but on burial, she was firm and resisted all of our attempts to dissuade her.

A filial son, Father had always respected Grandma's wishes and seldom argued with her in front of us. This was different. At dinner, he talked for the sake of Grandma about how Communist leaders Chairman Mao and Premier Zhou Enlai had embraced the idea of cremation back in the 1950s. "If our great leaders don't even ask for exceptions, what's so special about us?" After attending a coworker's funeral at Sanzhao Crematorium, in the southern part of the city, he told her, "It wasn't bad." The body of the deceased was brought over; relatives, friends, and coworkers gathered for a brief wake. Instead of the traditional sutra chanting and wailing, sad yet upbeat Communist-style mourning music played over a loudspeaker. Government or company officials delivered eulogies; family members thanked the officials and gave brief talks. After everyone bid good-bye, the body was slid into a furnace and the ashes were gathered at the other end and placed in a cinerary urn, which was taken to a big hall, like a library. Important leaders were accorded a bigger memorial service, and they didn't have to wait in line for the furnace, but everyone went the same way. On Qingming, or Tomb-Sweeping Day, relatives retrieved the urn and paid tribute to the deceased in a big yard behind the crematorium.

Grandma was skeptical. Neighbors had told her how crematorium workers never completely emptied out the furnaces after each cremation. "When they scoop out handfuls of ashes from inside the furnace, how would you know they're mine? You might pay tribute to someone else's mother at Qingming." Grandma ended the conversation by standing and clearing the table.

Mother couldn't bear to see her husband beaten so easily. "Where do you expect us to bury you? Have you ever seen a cemetery around here? What makes you think your husband's tomb is still there in Henan?"

Grandma dismissed her with the wave of a hand. "I'm sure the Huang family maintains the tomb and they have kept a place for me." She made it clear to Father that she would be buried in her native village with a traditional funeral, and that she would not be denied her last request.

2.

VENERATION

As one of the few survivors of wars, floods, and famine in the pre-Communist era, Grandma was always venerated in our neighborhood. On the first day of the Lunar New Year, while most of my classmates got to sleep in after a night of firecrackers, Mother woke us before sunrise, had us dressed in new clothes, and rushed us through breakfast, shouting, "Hurry up and eat your dumplings . . . people will be here any moment."

Then neighbors and friends would stream in early in the morning to wish Grandma a happy New Year. They believed that some of her longevity might rub off on them if they started their year by visiting her. Grandma would sit on her bed at the far end

of the living room, a new quilt covering her feet and legs, looking fresh in her baggy navy blue shirt with buttons down the side,
a black velvet hat on her head. She would nod and beam as our
guests described her as a "faithful widow" and complimented her
for raising a big family like ours.

"Huang Mama, your sufferings and sacrifices haven't gone
wasted," they would shout into her ear. "Look at your family—
it's a full house with four grandchildren. They will grow up to
honor you and take good care of you."

A couple of times, with her eyes glistening, she'd respond,
"Let me tell you, it wasn't easy!"

Our neighbors, especially Mother's female friends, made a
big thing of Grandma's being a "faithful widow." It was true that
Grandpa had died a long time ago and that Grandma had never
remarried, but her widowhood never struck me as anything
unusual. Families portrayed in revolutionary propaganda movies
always had a tough, gray-haired grandma figure wearing a loose
blue garment with buttons on the side and patched-up holes on
the sleeves. Of course, in the movies she would be a fervent revolutionary who faced the enemy guns heroically to protect her
children and other comrades. There was never a grandpa.

In the spring of 1974, on a class field trip to a village outside
Xi'an, some friends and I came across a crumbling stone arch
with faded Chinese characters standing lonely amid piles of garbage. My teacher said it was a chastity arch from the nineteenth
century, erected in honor of a young widow who remained faithful to her husband after his death. My teacher pointed out that
it was a testimony to the suffering and oppression of women in

feudalistic society, where they were regarded as "possessions." Noticing that we looked baffled, she explained by citing a different story, which was a familiar plot in traditional opera.

In the city of Suzhou during the sixteenth century, a young woman lost her husband. Grief-stricken, she vowed to take care of her in-laws and make raising her son her sole purpose in life so that her husband's bloodline could continue. However, her loneliness became too much to bear, and she flirted with her son's tutor who turned her down out of righteousness and lectured her on the importance of being faithful. Ashamed of her lapse, she chopped off two of her fingers to express her remorse and determination that her son should come first. In the end, her son passed the imperial exam and rose to a high government position. Touched by her story, the emperor crowned her a noble mother and she became an example for other women to follow, sustaining a rigid Confucian moral code that put men before women and deprived women of happiness.

"Confucian moral code" meant little to me, but the story sounded a lot like Grandma's life, though my father never attained a senior government position and Grandma never received any recognition as a noble mother from Chairman Mao. I wanted to learn more about Grandma's life, of which I had heard only fragments. In the evenings, after I was done with homework, I would beg her for stories. She was at first a little surprised and embarrassed, perhaps even suspicious, that I was suddenly interested in her story. "There is nothing to tell," she would say. "It was so long ago and I don't remember." But when she was in the right mood, she would let herself wander and tell a story. I became entranced by her Henan accent. Sometimes she kept talking long after I had fallen asleep.

Grandma was born in the Year of the Tiger, which comes every twelve years and, knowing that, my sister Wenxia and I calculated that it must have been 1902. My sister had rummaged through Father's files and found our family registration document, which listed her birthday as April 14. Grandma said she made that up because people in the rural areas didn't pay much attention to a girl's birthday when she was young. When she arrived in Xi'an, the Public Security Bureau wouldn't accept that as an excuse so she plucked a date out of the air. "It's a lucky thing not to remember your birthday—you can live forever," she said.

Her parents were farmers in a village in Wen County in northwest Henan. They owned some land, which seemed the standard to measure one's family wealth. Her only childhood memory involved the binding of her feet. She was six when her mother began wrapping her feet tightly with cotton bandages. A younger sister began the same ordeal four years later, even though the practice was banned when the revolutionaries toppled the Qing Dynasty in 1912. Grandma said the most insulting thing that could be said about a woman was "She has ugly big feet."

"Most well-to-do families would bind their daughters' feet," she said. "With big feet, a girl would never find a husband." The first three months were excruciatingly painful, even though her mother claimed that the bones in her feet were soft and relatively easy to bend inward without having to break them. Grandma could scarcely leave her bed and passed the time learning to sew and knit. Her feet became badly infected, so each time her mother rewrapped her feet, she would put thin shards of porcelain against Grandma's soles, tighten the bandages, and make her walk around to drive the shards into her flesh. The idea was that drawing off the blood and pus would make her feet even smaller. Grandma would sometimes pass out from the pain, but her mother would not relent. After soaking Grandma's feet in herbal water, her mother would put the bandages back on, tighter than before. "I cried a lot," she said. A lifetime later, her feet are wrapped with strips of wide cloth in the morning and unwrapped at night, though in winter she often left the strips on for extra warmth.

As a small boy, I shared Grandma's tiny bed, sleeping at the opposite end. I would sometimes clutch her tiny feet in my arms. Her toes bent inward, like tiny pieces of dough flattened by a rolling pin, the feet themselves pyramid shaped, like the pig trotters that Mother sometimes cooked.

Grandma said she had several suitors at the age of fifteen. Her family was cautious and, after much negotiation through a village matchmaker, settled on the Huang family, which owned a large swath of prime farmland along the Yellow River and lived in a big courtyard house. The Huang were descended from a military officer who served the Qing Emperor Tongzhi in the 1860s.

She was seventeen when she married, so long ago that she had no recollection of what Grandpa looked like on their wedding day. Photography had reached China's big cities but was unheard of in the countryside. When my sister pressed her about Grandpa's looks, she said he was "short, like your father, but had big eyes and pale skin." To her, big eyes and pale skin were the epitome of good looks. She acknowledged that Grandpa had a farmer's bad temper, something that flared in Father from time to time, but he treated her well. "Your Grandpa would pick some apples or apricots in the orchard, wrap them in his shirt, and bring them home for me," she said, which I took to mean, in her shy and roundabout way, that she was saying he loved her.

Everyone lived under the same roof, Grandma and Grandpa, his parents, his younger brother. Grandma gave birth to two boys. Father was born in 1928, the Year of the Dragon, traditionally an auspicious year but one that brought calamity to the family.

At the beginning of that year, a member of the Huang clan married a young woman from a wealthy family in a faraway village. "The dowry came in dozens of carts—clothing, bolts of fabric, quilts of silk, beautiful wooden cases, jewelry, several big horses." It seemed that the family had struck gold in what everyone said was a "perfect match." No one noticed the bride had also brought with her a cough, which worsened over time until she could scarcely breathe. A few months after the wedding, she died. Everyone said it was a tragedy, until her husband began coughing, too.

The bride had brought *laobing* into the village—tuberculosis. Soon Grandpa developed a cough. Instead of sending for a medical doctor, the Huang family consulted a local shaman, who prescribed the burning of incense. The shaman said a former tenant, who harbored grudges against my great-grandfather, had put a curse on the Huang family, and he tried to lift the curse with chanting and incense. Soon the house was so filled with smoke that it was suffocating.

The chanting and incense burning failed to save Grandpa, who died soon after. Grandpa had left word with his parents, saying that Grandma could remarry after his death, but if she did so, she would have to leave their two sons behind to be adopted by his brother and sister-in-law.

A feng shui master was summoned to find an auspicious spot for Grandpa's burial, one that would drive away the deadly cloud that seemed to hang over the Huang family. Perhaps the feng shui master took too long over his calculations, because on the day of Grandpa's burial my uncle collapsed at the cemetery. This time the family took him to a doctor who diagnosed him with TB. He died a month later at the age of eight. And so it went, until Father was the only surviving male of the Huang clan.

Grandma was only twenty-seven and had lost her husband and eldest son. She cried day and night; at one point, she claimed that she even lost her sight. She said that she thought of hanging herself, but my father was only four months old and she pitied him. Like a "faithful widow" in those ancient Chinese stories, she vowed to protect her son and continue the Huang family bloodline.

Father was raised in a house of widows. They banded together to share the running of the farm, hiring laborers to plant and harvest grain. They were difficult years, though there was still worse to come. In the summer of 1933, the Yellow River flooded. The dam that was supposed to protect the region collapsed and the whole region was submerged. Houses were destroyed; people and livestock drowned; everything of value was washed away. Grandma and Father climbed an old tree and waited three days for the water to recede. A relative told me that the county chief was an incompetent transplant from the south and had grossly underestimated the severity of the Yellow River flood. There was no flood relief, no rescue operations. Instead, he encouraged people to pray and promised a three-day opera festival if their prayers stopped the rain and stemmed the flood.

Disaster struck again in 1938 when invading Japanese troops marched into Henan, and the region was rife with bandits and Japanese collaborators who looted grain and livestock and robbed the villagers of their valuables. Without any men, the Huang family was an easy target. "Bandits broke into our house, snatching grain and valuables," Grandma said. "They used wooden sticks to knock on the floor and walls. If they heard any hollow sound, they would dig a hole to see if we had hidden anything.

"When a family is in decline, even the animals want to leave," she said. "We owned ten big horses. Before the Japanese troops arrived, we hid them in a secret garden behind the house. As the troops were passing, the horses started to whinny and the soldiers seized them all."

There was little food and the wheat never had a chance to ripen. Peasants picked the fields clean of wheatgrass, which they ground for juice or dried and ate as a powder. The family's priority was to keep Father nourished, often at the expense of everyone else.

Soon Grandma realized that the family would face starvation if they stayed put. She decided to take Father and make for a city in Shanxi Province, which meant walking several hundred kilometers on bound feet. Grandma's sewing skills served her well. During the day, Grandma made clothes for wealthy families; at night, she slept in an abandoned temple with her relatives and fellow villagers. When a wolf snatched away a three-year-old boy playing outside the temple at sunset, and all the adults could find were his bloodstained and tattered clothes, she and Father returned to her home village, which offered no sanctuary. In the spring of 1942, not a single raindrop fell in the region. Starvation was widespread. In the autumn, a plague of locusts ate everything that was left. Grandma said they lived on grass roots and tree bark. Others lived off the recently dead or the passing strangers they trapped, killed, and cooked. Half of the surviving Huang family died, including both her in-laws. Grandma took Father, who was now twelve, and fled Henan.

During the hardest times, Grandma and Father begged on the streets, until they contracted typhoid and lay racked by fever in an old crumbling temple. A woman living nearby saw them when they crawled out to beg and took pity on them, leaving food and drinking water each day for Grandma to find.

It was Xi'an, the capital city in the neighboring province of Shaanxi, that finally offered Grandma and Father a refuge. The invading Japanese never reached Xi'an. The fertile land and mild climate made a haven for Henan refugees. For a rural woman who had never seen a lightbulb, the big city was baffling. Through fellow villagers, Grandma found work as a maid to the owner of a large jewelry store, Mr. Ren, who needed help looking after the children of his wife and his concubines. Grandma and Father moved into a small one-room house adjacent to a spacious courtyard mansion in the eastern section of the city. Grandma cooked, washed clothes, and nursed Ren's children. I remember Grandma as a proud woman, and I asked how she handled the transition from sheltered daughter of a wealthy rural family to a maid. "I did it for my son," she said. "Only a parent would understand."

Grandma gained a reputation as a tough and capable woman, but there were limits. When one of Ren's concubines accused her of stealing a gold ring, Grandma grew angry in her denial, mortified by the attack on her character, and the concubine slapped her so hard she fell unconscious to the ground. Rather than leave, Grandma stood her ground. Three days later, the concubine found the ring, which she had simply misplaced. She never apologized. Whenever Grandma talked about the incident, her bottom lip would tremble. She and Father lived under Ren's protection for fourteen years, raising five of his children. The job provided an anchor for my teenage father who was eager to start out on his own, working during the day and attending school at night.

When the Communist government was established in 1949, all their suffering turned out to be a blessing. Grandma and Father were classified as poor peasants, true proletariats, and all the opportunities of the new society were open to them. Father was given a job at a textile factory. In the late 1950s, the government took over Ren's jewelry stores and he became an employee. He could no longer pay for Grandma's help, but Father had a stable income and she felt it was time to retire as a maid.

In 1956, Father married a woman who grew up not far from his native village and had been brought to Xi'an by her aunt. The woman was my mother. Father was twenty-eight then, but Grandma never let go of him. They all lived together inside a tiny two-bedroom house in Ren's courtyard. When my older sister and I were born, Grandma took it as a sign that the Huang family might again prosper. She took care of us when Mother was away at work.

Often, to the frustration of Father, Grandma never showed any interest in the revolution that had ended her suffering and the subsequent political campaigns against those who had exploited her. Instead, she always blamed the family's hardships on her own fate and the vengeful ghost of a former tenant who, she said, had placed a curse on the family.

In 1966, at the outset of the Cultural Revolution, Red Guards took over Ren's courtyard house, confiscated all his possessions, and pushed his family into a corner room. The rest of the house was opened up to families of revolutionary activists. Grandma, a member of the oppressed and exploited proletariat, was offered a bigger room in the mansion and was asked to speak against her former boss at public denunciation meetings. Grandma declined both offers and insisted on staying in her little room. The Red Guards didn't know what to do about this illiterate old lady with bound feet, this ally of the revolution. When Ren was paraded through the streets, Grandma secretly took care of his children. "After all, I had raised them like they were my own," she said.

When I was in elementary school, Grandma constantly embarrassed me in front of my friends. My elder sister and I participated in different kinds of after-school music performances and parades to promote the latest Party policies. Grandma would wobble outside and look for us. When we appeared, she let us have it in her richest Henan accent. "You goof off outside after school, doing this revolution and that revolution, but never bother to come home and take care of your brother and sister. What kind of crap is that?" She made such a ruckus that many of our friends had come out to watch and they were all laughing. We were mortified. From then on, classmates would mimic Grandma's actions and accent to tease us.

In high school, I was taught that a Communist society meant that there would be fewer differences in wealth, power, and status. Everyone would have all the food and clothing they needed. Nobody would be selfish. We would all want to work hard and help others. When I shared these sentiments with Grandma, she laughed at me and mocked my Communist faith. "That's the perfect dream for a lazy person like you." She wrinkled her nose. "Just who will provide the food and clothing that everyone needs? They don't fall from the sky, do they?" Grandma's sarcasm made me angry, and I told Father what she had said. Father gave me a serious look and said, "Don't listen to your grandma and don't tell others what she says. She is illiterate and backward in thinking." As I left the room, I heard him tell Grandma, "Watch out. He doesn't know any better and could talk to his friends. If they report us to the authorities, they might think those were my ideas." It was true. A neighbor's child shared with his classmates that his grandpa had said that most of the landlords that had been executed by the government were diligent and kindhearted people. A few days later, his father, the personnel director, was under investigation for attacking the government's Land Reform Movement.

Grandma never changed what my siblings called "her backward and nonrevolutionary ways of thinking." After reading the story about the faithful widow, I asked Grandma if she felt she was a victim of reviled Confucianism by being forced to remain a widow all her life. I was hoping she would condemn the oppressive feudalistic system and praise the liberation of women under Communism. What I got was a look that showed she thought I was crazy. "What did I have to do with Confucius? I didn't want my son to be mistreated by a stepfather. That was all."

I turned to Father who, to my surprise, agreed with Grandma. "She sacrificed for my sake," he said. A merchant from Henan once had expressed interest in Grandma when they first arrived in Xi'an. He had proposed several times through a matchmaker. Many of her friends and relatives tried to persuade her to consider his offer. "With a man in the family, it's easier to raise a son and you don't have to work as hard," they said. Grandma did not relent. She was always careful about her reputation too. Mother thought the story good enough to spread around, with the unintended result that respect for Grandma went even higher. Looking back, I saw two subtly different reactions. When men praised her, it was about her sacrifice "for the sake of your father and family—so rare in these days." While women admired her devotion, they also sympathized. "Can you imagine how tough it was for a young widow to take care of a boy all by herself? Treat her nicely."

Thus, when Grandma talked to other elderly women in our neighborhood about her burial plan, none thought it excessive. Those to whom Father confided his dilemma—close friends at work, mostly men, and a few relatives—urged prudence.

A distant grandnephew of Grandma's and a regular at our house strongly opposed Grandma's idea; we respected his advice because he had joined the Party at twenty-three and had embarked on a promising political career. "It would be a big political blunder," he warned. "The ban is quite strict. You could get into serious trouble. Why don't you promise Grandma a burial now and then do whatever you want to do after she passes away."

"If I did that," Father said, "Grandma's ghost would come back to haunt me the rest of my life. She's a tough woman and I owe my life to her."

3.

DILEMMA

Grandma's request presented a dilemma for Father, who felt obligated to give Grandma the burial she wanted but feared for his political future. For many years, Father had been a poster child for the Chinese Communist Party, having been voted model Party member at his workplace several years in a row. His black-and-white photograph was a regular feature on the company's bulletin board. And every year on July 1, the day that marks the founding of the Chinese Communist Party, he would be presented with a red certificate at an all-staff meeting or sometimes coworkers would beat gongs and drums all the way to our house to deliver the honor.

In today's China, red certificates mean nothing—cash-stuffed red envelopes at year's end are what count—but things were different then. Bonuses were a capitalistic practice that corrupted the soul and lacked honor. Father had his certificates framed and they hung within view of the front door. Grandma was unimpressed and, in her disdain for the impractical, muttered: "What good are they? Can you exchange them for steamed buns?" But realizing that she had offended Father, she conceded that red was a lucky color and that the certificates did look nice on the drab white walls.

Membership in the Party involved not only embracing its ideology and policies but also having oneself held to a higher moral standard. Party members were supposed to work harder, inspire leadership, and live harmoniously with their families. The Party idealized its members and the people did so too.

Father was a warehouse manager, which sounds grander than it was; he was more a warehouse keeper. He worked for a state-run company that manufactured cast-iron cookware and industrial water pipes. There was coal and lead dust everywhere in the factory, and it spread to the trees and rooftops. Workers coming out of the workshops looked like coal miners, their faces and hands smeared with soot from the cast-iron molds. Father only needed to visit the workshops once a day to check up on the quantities of cooking utensils. His face and overalls were clean. I used to visit his office after school and do my homework there. He always seemed to be hunched over in the backs of trucks, checking the quantity of cooking utensils loaded against the quantity ordered and tallying it against incoming and outgoing shipments. Often, the lines of trucks lasted all day, and once they were gone, he had to reconcile the books. He never complained.

When my political-study teacher was looking for a speaker who could talk about the "bitterness" of life before the revolution and how much better things were in the new socialist society, I volunteered Father. I had heard him talk about those years, though I was still nervous because any gaffes would be magnified by my classmates and used to torment me. I was afraid that, like Grandma, he might blame the hardships on the vengeful ghost.

Father was well prepared. A manager at his company's propaganda department drafted a script that made it clear which regime to condemn and which to praise. The teacher said afterward that Father's story was just what she wanted.

This was how Father described his early years. He was born on December 16, 1928, according to the Chinese lunar calendar. He told us how, at an early age, he lost his father and other relatives to the TB epidemic. He pointed out that rural folks did not have access to education and were ignorant of modern medicine, relying on shamans and incense instead. China's backward public-health system lacked the basic capacity to stem the epidemic.

According to Father, his home village relied on a rich region of loess, good for wheat and peanuts, but flood and drought brought much sorrow. It was the 1942 famine that turned him into a fervent supporter of the Communists. He was fourteen, and the drought had created a severe food shortage. Local officials continued to levy their taxes, and grain reserves and livestock were sold to satisfy their demands. The famine and the ensuing locust plague killed more than three million people, aided by the Japanese invasion of Henan and the looting and burning of villages and the rape of women. In many places, peasants collaborated with the Japanese invaders because they were so fed up with the corrupt Nationalist government. Father and Grandma joined the other famine refugees walking west. The dead and dying were everywhere. Father didn't tell of the gangs who killed and ate lone strangers on the road, but he did mention that a family, no longer strong enough to push their two boys and a girl ahead of them in a wheelbarrow, lifted their daughter out and left her by the road. They begged Grandma to take her, as a maid or a daughter, but her sole responsibility was Father and she walked on. Tears welled up in his eyes as he told how the little girl had been left to die.

"At this point, one would assume that government officials would realize the extent of the emergency and would rush in with food supplies to help the refugees," Father said to my class. "But no, the corrupt Nationalists were too busy helping themselves to what was left before running away from the Japanese, and then they went looting, too. It was hopeless," Father said. "Without Chairman Mao and the Party, we would still be eating tree bark." There was a degree of stiffness to Father's delivery of that line and I could tell the part was written by the propaganda manager. Having lived through humiliating poverty in his childhood, Father said he embraced Chairman Mao's promise of a new society built on equality and plenty.

"When I was your age, I couldn't afford to go to school," he said. "I was envious of children who could sit in brightly lit classrooms and read books without worrying about food and shelter."

He recalled how close to death he and Grandma were in the abandoned temple as they lay stricken with typhoid. I stole a glance at my teacher and saw the light reflect a tear in the corner of each eye.

While researching this book, I looked up the 1942 famine. It was true that the Nationalist government, which was preoccupied with war with Japan, acted indifferently, and its rescue efforts were slow in coming. About three million people perished in the famine. However, between 1959 and 1961, the famine caused by Chairman Mao's radical policies led to the death of an estimated thirty to forty million people. With the Party's relentless blocking of news and information, there was no way Father could know about it.

In front of the whole class, Father declared how much better things were for us, how our lives had been changed for the better under Communism, how even his own family of seven could have two bicycles, two Red Flag–brand watches, a sewing machine, and a two-bedroom apartment. He even mentioned a giant mahogany armoire that he had bought for five yuan at a sale organized by the company's Revolutionary Committee, which had confiscated furniture and other valuables from capitalists and counterrevolutionaries during the Cultural Revolution.

At the end of Father's speech, my teacher led a vigorous round of applause. Though my classmates mimicked his Henan accent, Father's talk made a huge impression.

When Father told my classmates about his life as a poor peasant in the pre-Communist era, he left out the fact that his family had been wealthy landowners. In Mother's words, "The

Huang family was lucky to have lost all its fortune in the flood, war, and famine. Otherwise, you could have been standing on the stage with a big dunce cap to receive public denunciation rather than lecturing other young people." Father never mentioned the fact that at the age of eleven, his family had arranged a marriage for him to a sixteen-year-old woman. Child marriage, a sign of old society, had long been outlawed in Communist China. Father's marriage took place right after Japan had invaded China. Young women in well-to-do families would either marry or smear their faces with soot and dirt to hide their looks so that the Japanese soldiers at the checkpoints would not see them as beautiful young virgins and rape them. A matchmaker fixed up Father with that woman from a nearby village. Grandma, eager to see her son establish a family, consented. A small perfunctory ceremony was held and the woman moved in with the Huang family. A year later, as tales of Japanese brutality against young married women reached the village, Grandma sent Father's wife home for fear that they wouldn't be able to protect her properly. The marriage dissolved. In fact, Father had never shared this episode with Mother. I found out about it during a recent trip to his native village, long after he had died.

More important, Father hardly talked about life in his twenties and thirties. One of his colleagues once hinted that Father used to be a laborer. I couldn't reconcile myself to the image of Father pulling long wooden carts filled with cooking utensils. In our family album, there was a portrait of a young handsome Father wearing a western-style turtleneck, his hair neatly parted on one side. He said the photo was taken on his twenty-fifth birthday. He looked more like a scholar than a laborer. His body seemed too delicate, his mind too sophisticated. Most laborers at Father's company were illiterate and wore dirty uniforms and talked crudely, while Father was well versed in Chinese literature and tradition, and was sharp with his abacus. I asked him several times if he had really been a laborer. He evaded the question by saying, "I'll tell you when you grow up."

In 1984, Father and I went on a trip together. On the long train ride, he opened up to me about his past. It was like a sequel to his "speak bitterness" session with my class, but more honest, more revealing.

After the Communist takeover in 1949, Father joined a textile factory. He worked during the day and attended night school. Father would always credit the Communists with giving him the liberating experience of being able to read and write. Within a few years, he read all the major Chinese literary classics, and enjoyed movies and opera. The Party noticed Father's diligence and he was moved to the government's cultural bureau.

Father truly viewed the Party as an elite group of the best in society and he longed to be part of it. To become a member is a long, rigorous process, and to help his application, Father became actively involved in every political campaign. During the Great Leap Forward, when Chairman Mao hatched an ambitious plan to industrialize the nation within a short time, Father and his coworkers spent days and nights at work, with only a few hours of sleep every day. He truly believed that China could produce enough iron and steel to fight the Western economic embargo against Communist China by using only makeshift furnaces. "We were such a large country. If we could beat the United States in Korea, we would surely be successful with industrialization. We were so confident," he said. At the height of what he called his youthful passion and enthusiasm, he submitted his first application for Party membership. It was 1958.

"I was young, enthusiastic, outspoken, and reckless," he said. And, by his tone, he might have added "foolish." At the beginning of 1959, the local Party secretary encouraged young people to voice criticism against Party officials to help them improve. Father took him at his word and said the Party secretary should be more open to the suggestions of others. He was too "dictatorial." Father believed the Party secretary sincerely appreciated the criticism and had even noted it down. But for days after, there was coldness in the Party secretary's attitude toward him, and not long after this, Father was informed that the Party needed him to launch a literacy project in a mountainous village in the northern part of Shaanxi Province. Father knew it was retaliation for his outspokenness. Two months into the assignment, he received a telegram from Grandma, who had fallen down a flight of stairs and seriously injured her legs. He rushed home to care for her and returned to the village after her condition had stabilized. When Father was accused by the Party secretary of putting his family ahead of the revolution, he was sacked.

Being jobless in 1960 was not a good situation to be in; famine caused by Chairman Mao's Great Leap Forward campaign began to spread nationwide. Food rations were cut in urban areas, and

Father was stripped of his government food subsidies. Mother's income was low and the family savings were soon exhausted buying food on the black market. He picked up odd jobs at shoe-repair stands on the street, and on weekends he would bike Grandma out of the city to pick over harvested fields for loose cabbage leaves. The Communist Party hid its mistakes by blaming the famine on drought and Father easily accepted what he was told. Even so, it was a humiliating experience for him and others. "You can't believe how desperate people became," he said. A middle-aged man neatly dressed in a Maoist uniform passed him on a bicycle and stopped a little farther on. The man got off his bike, bent down, and picked up something from the ground. Father assumed it was a coin, but as he drew closer, he saw that it was a discarded pear stem. The man put it in his mouth and, sucking on it greedily, slowly peddled away. "People developed edema, and their faces and legs were all swollen. Some fell to the ground and died," he said.

In 1964, a friend had helped secure him a job at a cookware company. It was a laborer's job, loading and unloading cast-iron cooking utensils and pulling a huge wooden cart. This was after I was born. He didn't think he was strong enough to handle the tough work, but with two children and a mother to support, he had no real choice.

The sacking and his experience as an unemployed young person in the subsequent famine of 1960 diminished Father's belief in the Party and damaged his confidence. "I learned a valuable lesson about keeping my mouth shut," Father said. Fortunately, he got off lightly. Though Father lost his job for his act of criticism, it wasn't classified as a political case. In addition, the offended Party secretary was ousted at the beginning of the Cultural Revolution, when Chairman Mao mobilized millions of young people, known as the Red Guards, to attack government officials and intellectuals and seize power from those whom Mao believed had strayed from the path of Communism. Several years later, Father's name was cleared and he received a small sum of money as compensation for lost wages. He was asked to return to his job in the cultural bureau, but he no longer understood what was happening in that sphere and felt safer as a worker.

Father's affability and his diligence served him well at his new job. He soon moved up to be in charge of the company's warehouse. At the height of the Cultural Revolution, Father was a spectator rather than a participant. He showed up at work every day and tried to maintain amicable relations with all sides as the company's employees split into factions, each accusing the other of betraying Communist principle as they fought for control of the company. Father's proletariat background and his low status as an ordinary worker shielded him from assault as he sat back and watched verbal warfare turn physical. Each faction took over a building and started shooting at the other with handmade guns. No one did any work.

In 1969, the situation in Xi'an settled down, political lines became somewhat more stable and work resumed. Father's fortunes seemed to be taking a turn for the better. Around that time, Chairman Mao pushed to purify the ranks of the Communist Party by recruiting ordinary workers and peasants. The attention of the Party leadership fell on Father. I like to think it was because he did nothing in times of political turmoil and made few enemies. He was asked to apply for Party membership. Mother opposed the move, worrying that he could be burned again. Father was hopeful. Membership was good for his career and the children. Father drafted an application essay about his past sufferings under the Nationalist regime, his gratitude to Chairman Mao and the Party, how he viewed the Party as the vanguard of the working class, and how he felt inspired to serve the Party. Since he never liked his own handwriting, he had me copy the statements neatly on a brand-new template that he had gotten from the company's Party Organization Department. After laboring over them for hours, I showed them to Father. He examined them and shook his head. "Your handwriting doesn't look sophisticated enough," he said. Eventually, he enlisted the help of the company's newscaster whose shrill voice could be heard on the loudspeaker, reading editorials from the Communist Party newspaper every day at lunch.

Soon an official at the propaganda department tipped off Father that the leadership was considering his application. The Party assigned him a sponsor, who would conduct a talk with Father to gauge his political thinking every month and point out areas for improvement. Nine months after Father submitted his application, two Party officials were dispatched to conduct background checks at Father's native village. Letters were sent to former employers and neighborhood committees soliciting feedback. The dangled promise of Party membership was coming within reach.

One day, a company official took him aside and explained there had been a "hiccup" in the process. The company had received an anonymous letter from a neighbor who accused Father of selling shoes on the black market during the famine in 1961. It was a serious allegation. Using the black market was an illegal capitalistic practice. Father explained that he had worked for a time with a shoe repairman after he was fired from his former employer, but he never sold shoes on the black market.

It was not until much later that Father learned the name of the complainant—Mr. Ren, the jewelry-store owner, who had held a grudge against him since the start of the Cultural Revolution because Father had rebuked him at public meetings for exploiting and mistreating Grandma when she worked as his maid. Further investigation, which involved talking to more people in the neighborhood, verified Father's explanation. That the defamatory letter was written by a former capitalist and was aimed at a "revolutionary worker" sealed the case.

In 1972, Father became a member of the Chinese Communist Party, fulfilling a wish that he had held since 1958. On the day of the announcement, one of Father's colleagues brought me to the meeting room. We stood outside and peeked in from a window. I saw him raise his right arm and pledge his loyalty to Chairman Mao and the Party. The Party membership rekindled his hope in life and brought him unexpected benefits. A year later, Father's company, noting his good work record, assigned him a large unit in a newly built apartment complex adjacent to the company— in reality, six tightly packed rows of drab tenements with mud walls and redbrick edges.

Everything we owned fit into a truck, which drove us from Ren's old courtyard through noisy, crowded downtown Xi'an to a developing northern suburb. We were one of the first families to arrive. The place was deserted. Grandma's pride in her son's success turned to panic when she learned that the residential complex was built on an old execution ground where criminals and counterrevolutionaries were shot. She feared their ghosts. We children faced our own challenges. In the city, there was the constant danger of getting lost. Here, there were wolves. We were taught never to leave the house after dark and, in an emergency, how to use a flashlight to ward off attacks by wolf packs. There was no indoor plumbing and the public latrines were two blocks distant. It was like living on an island in a sea of wheat fields and collective farms. Grandma called our house "a cave in the boondocks." Even so, Mother saw it as a big improvement over our cramped apartment in the city.

After we had moved to our new place, Father's political fortune continued to rise. A "progressive worker" and "model Communist Party member," he was elected as a delegate to the district Party Congress and his name even appeared in the local newspaper.

With his newly gained political status, Father said he was deeply torn between his loyalties to the Party and his mother. He was afraid that arranging a traditional burial for Grandma in Henan would erase all the honors he had painstakingly accrued within the Party.

As Grandma became more vocal and persistent, Father became more withdrawn. He seldom talked at dinner. Sometimes, when I woke in the night, I could hear him murmuring to Mother about Grandma. He later admitted that Grandma's death had always weighed on his mind, long before she had turned seventy-two.

He had relied on the Chinese saying that "the cart will find its way around the mountain when it gets closer," and he hoped that the issue would resolve itself. Now, he was being forced to act. In those trying months, his hair had started to turn gray.

Eventually he went to one particular friend, Li Haoshan, to seek advice. Li, a former government official, was removed from office by the Red Guards in 1969. After they locked him in a detention center, Father snuck him food and blankets while everyone else deserted him. In 1973, the government reversed its verdict against him and he resumed his leadership position at the city's Light Industry Bureau, the agency that regulated Father's company. "You are taking a big risk in granting your mother's final wish," he said, jokingly. "If this had been in the old days, you would have been written into the book of filial children." Li promised to cover for Father if anything went wrong, though he doubted there would be a problem. "Your mother used to be a poor and illiterate maid, and your family background is clean and pure," he said. "They'll probably let you get away with it." Li indicated that if Grandma's body was shipped to another province, as was planned, Father's company would not have jurisdiction. In any event, he doubted Father would get more than a letter of self-criticism. Li's suggestions emboldened Father. He was ready to make a plan.

4.

OBLIGATION

Before Lunar New Year in 1974, a colleague who reported to Father at the company warehouse was planning to visit his native village during the long holiday. He was from the same part of Henan as the Huang family and his trip gave Father an idea. He asked the colleague to deliver a letter and a gift of blue cloth to a cousin of Grandpa's, who lived in a village not far from where the colleague was going. In the letter, Father inquired about Grandpa's tomb and sounded out the cousin on the possibility of Grandma being buried there, too.

We treated Father's colleague like a long-lost uncle when he showed up at our house a month later. He had brought back a bottle of peanut oil, a specialty of the region, and a verbal message from Grandpa's cousin—Grandpa's tomb was intact and it would not be a problem for Grandma to be buried there. Grandma was thrilled, but Father remained unconvinced.

"The local government is under pressure to impose bans on burial," the colleague reported. "But village people, especially older folks, are still traditional and they are resisting the order." He said Grandpa's cousin seemed to be a powerful figure, and so long as we could get Grandma's body to him and keep the funeral low-key, it would be okay.

"It is a big taboo to leave your father buried alone," the colleague advised before he left. "Uniting our parents in death is a time-honored custom in our hometown and it's good for the future of the family." He admitted that it would not be acceptable to bring Grandma's ashes home for a joint burial. "It doesn't count," he added.

Grandma seized on the colleague's report as proof that her request should be respected. She had recruited other old women in our neighborhood to pressure Father into agreeing to the burial. "Considering what she has gone through for you, you certainly don't want to deny her last request," they said.

As time went by, Father realized that he was engaging in a losing battle. With warmer weather came Father's final decision. One night after dinner, he had us stay at the table. He seemed to be in a jovial and chatty mood, and told a story that bewildered us initially because it was not related to any topics that we had discussed that evening.

"Sun Zhong grew watermelons and diligently served his aging

parents. One hot summer day, three gray-bearded men passed his field, searching for water. Sun offered them a large watermelon, which they ate quickly and with relish, slurping up the juice and not letting a drop fall. They asked for more. Sun brought a bigger one from his field and he refused to take their money. Touched by the young man's generosity, the strangers decided to give him a gift. One of the old men said to Sun, 'I'm going to reveal a good feng shui spot. You should continue to take good care of your parents, and when they die, bury them at this spot. If you do this, there will be an emperor in your family.' Sun was skeptical, but paid attention and when one of the men ordered him to walk up the hill—'Don't stop until I tell you'—he did as he was told. After about one hundred steps, he turned to see what the three strangers were up to in his field. The scholar sighed. '*Aiya*, you turned your head too early. Just stop where you are. The feng shui is also good there, but instead of an emperor, you will have a king who will rule in the south.' As Sun marked the spot, he saw the three men turn into white cranes and fly away. Sun Zhong was more attentive to his parents, and after they died, he buried them where the three old men had advised. He married a young woman in the village. They had a son. His name was Sun Jian, who later ruled the kingdom of Wu."

Father then issued his usual disclaimer. "This is an old fable, of course. We are living in a new society now and no longer believe in feng shui and other superstitions." We knew that he was committed to fulfilling Grandma's final wish that she be buried. "We do this for the future of our family," he told us. "More importantly, it is about paying back Grandma's hard work. She has sacrificed much for our family. It is our turn to make some sacrifices for her. We are going to find a way."

"Do you think the good location of Grandpa's tomb will make me a powerful man when I grow up?" I asked.

"It depends on you," Father said. "If you are a filial grandson at home and generous with others at school, the magic will work. You might grow up to be somebody."

That story had a tremendous influence on me. Even now, each time a street person, especially a gray-bearded man or a ragged old lady, approaches me for money, I always wonder if the person is a saint or a fairy in disguise to test my generosity. I will offer some money, hoping they could turn into cranes and fly away with their blessing. When I ignore a beggar's plea, I am hit with a fleeting sense of guilt, worrying about possible retribution.

Meanwhile, as if to underscore the urgency of our plan, Grandma fell ill in the spring. She suffered from severe dizzy spells that left her nauseated for hours. At first, we were not too concerned; Grandma had high blood pressure, which she blamed on my older sister, a tomboy who constantly upset her by getting into fights. Each time a dizzy spell hit her, she would be treated by a Dr. Gao, who headed the company's medical clinic. I had heard that Dr. Gao, who had graduated from the prestigious Beijing Medical College, was assigned to Father's company because his parents who were university professors had "political" problems during the Cultural Revolution.

"Mama Huang, your pulse is strong as ever," Dr. Gao said to Grandma. "You'll live a long time. In the meantime, take the pills I prescribe, and you'll feel much better." It was my job to run to the clinic and get the prescription filled. When she forgetfully took double the prescribed dosage, I ran to Dr. Gao's apartment, afraid for her life. "Don't worry. There is no danger. Simply ask your Grandma to drink lots of water." I learned later that the pills that sustained Grandma were merely vitamin B and C supplements.

Her condition was different this time. Grandma soon developed a fever that persisted and Dr. Gao put her on a course of antibiotics, but when that didn't work, he suggested a trip to the hospital just in case. Father disliked hospitals and thought the long trip across town and the interminable wait in the emergency room would only worsen her condition. On the recommendation of a coworker, he went to see a Dr. Xu, who was not really a doctor but an expert in traditional medicine who had been branded by the government as a "charlatan." He was not allowed to practice medicine and worked as a technician for a clothing manufacturer. But he had four children and practiced traditional medicine on the side to supplement his paltry salary.

Xu came to our house, took Grandma's pulse, examined her tongue and eyes, and diagnosed *shanghuo*—too much heat—which was fuelling infections inside her body. He jotted down a list of herbs, which were to be boiled in a clay pot. Charged with getting Grandma her medicine, I went to a state-run herbal store, which smelled musky. Tall glass jars filled shelves that reached the ceiling and contained what looked like dried plants and unidentifiable pieces of things, though I thought some of them looked like horns of some sort of creatures. I watched as the shop assistant brought down roots and grasses that I had not seen before.

They were weighed, crushed, and mixed into six small packets that were tied together with a piece of brown string. For six nights, Father emptied the contents of a packet into a small clay pot of water, which was left to bubble for a couple of hours on a small coal stove. The resulting concoction filled a small bowl to the brim. Grandma would drink it, grimacing as she swallowed.

The illness drained Grandma's strength, but not her will. Certain that she was dying, Grandma pleaded that Father should accelerate her burial planning. She was convinced Father would bow to Party pressure and follow her grandnephew's suggestion, which was to dump her in a furnace as soon as she was cold.

There was no hiding the pungent smell of the herbs, and it wasn't long before the querulous Mrs. Zhang, whose strong Henan accent I had often heard documenting her litany of woes, stopped by for a visit. She lived four doors down from our house. My parents tended to avoid her. Several times a day, we children were treated to her loud crude swearing as she rebuked her morose husband for this or that transgression. I wasn't prepared for the "sweet" Mrs. Zhang who bustled past me through the door and pulled my parents into her embrace, whispering softly with her gestures. Mrs. Zhang was the first person outside our family to talk about having a coffin made and preparing a set of shou-yi—burial clothing—to drive away the evil spirits that had made Grandma ill. Mrs. Zhang, then in her fifties, turned out to be something of an expert. In the past, she said it was common for children to prepare coffins for their elderly parents while they were still alive. Her own grandfather had purchased a coffin after turning sixty and each year added a layer of black paint on his birthday. He lived into his eighties. Mrs. Zhang was from the same region as Grandma and familiar with the old traditions and customs and so, on this if not on any other sensitive issue, Father put his trust in her hands.

Ironically, our neighbors, including Mrs. Zhang, studiously attended all kinds of political meetings that aimed to stamp out superstitious activities, but in private few practiced what the Party preached. People would cover some transgression by saying it was an old Henan or Xi'an custom. "Bad luck to violate." So, when Mrs. Zhang stepped forward and proposed we prepare a coffin for Grandma, no one thought her idea preposterous.

In recent years, coffins have transcended their dark connotation of death and become a lucky symbol for the living. Chinese officials and wealthy businessmen purchase miniature gold-plated coffins and display them prominently in offices as auspicious decorations. However, in the 1970s, buying a coffin for a living person in the city was considered an act of defiance against Party policies and punishment could be severe. Father thought that if the coffin might in some way help Grandma to get well and offer her peace of mind, he was willing to take the risk.

I had seen those ominous-looking coffins at funerals in villages outside our residential compound. They struck me as outright scary. I understood the logic of planning and sharing the work— Mother would prepare school supplies for me years before I needed them, and she was often part of a sewing circle that made beautiful quilts for the daughters of friends in anticipation of their marriages—but a coffin before Grandma's death?

Mrs. Zhang's coffin idea plunged my family into another round of fierce arguments, pitting Grandma against Mother. As usual, Father chose to remain silent even though he had already made up his mind.

Mother had promised earlier to honor Grandma's burial request, but secretly she clung to the hope that once Grandma died, she could persuade Father to change his mind. She knew very well that Father was fearful of authority and cherished his newly gained political status. Preparing a coffin would make the burial inevitable. She snapped at Father. "If you want to throw away your Party membership, please go ahead." Then, pointing to a neat stack of cartons that we used to store our clothes, Mother launched into an angry tirade: "We don't even have money to buy a wooden wardrobe for the living. What makes you think we can afford to have a big coffin made? With this small space, where are we going to place the coffin? In the kitchen?"

Grandma sat on her bed, sulking. When Mother stepped out of the room, she pointed a finger at Mother's back and grumbled. "Evil, evil! I know she can't wait to have me cremated after I die," she said. "I'm not going to let it happen. I want my coffin!" Father shook his head helplessly.

To the disappointment of Grandma, my elder sister and I also objected to the coffin idea. Grandma had raised both of us, and she had always counted on us to take her side during her fights with Mother. But this time we had important reasons to betray her. In addition to being frightened by the idea of storing a coffin in our house, both of us were facing major choices in our lives, the outcomes of which depended heavily on Father's strong political standing with the Party.

My elder sister was graduating from senior high school that year. Known for her math skills, she dreamed of attending a university and becoming a mathematician. In the early 1970s, the university system in China had just been reinstituted after Chairman Mao had abolished it at the beginning of the Cultural Revolution in 1966, condemning the universities as training grounds for bourgeois and counterrevolutionaries. Under the new system, universities would recruit only young workers, peasants, and soldiers who came from revolutionary families and were politically reliable. My sister considered herself a perfect candidate. She was a Red Guard and a member of the Communist Youth League. Too young to have beaten up their teachers and smashed temples and burned books, she and her classmates still wore red armbands and volunteered as traffic guards or helped peasants with the harvest. Two months before her graduation, my sister pledged at a Communist Youth League meeting to answer Chairman Mao's call and became a peasant in the remote parts of China. She saw her future in the countryside as both an adventure and a launching pad for her dream—with our impeccable proletariat family background, she would be eligible for university application.

I was facing a similar situation. A week before Mrs. Zhang's visit, the principal pulled me into her office and told me I had been selected by the school to compete for a place at the Xi'an Foreign Languages School. She reminded me that they were specifically targeting children of workers and peasants and, since students would be entrusted with the task of dealing with foreigners, it was important they came from a reliable revolutionary family.

When I shared the news with my parents, Mother burst out laughing, thinking the whole thing a joke. They had never heard anyone speak a foreign language, let alone me, a former stutterer. Father was concerned. In the 1950s, many people were urged to twist their tongues and learn Russian so we could communicate with the experts who came from the Soviet Union, our big socialist brother. When Nikita Khrushchev denounced many of Joseph Stalin's political purges, Chairman Mao called him a revisionist. The two countries almost went to war. People quickly abandoned their study of Russian.

My parents paid a visit to a friend's daughter who had been recruited to attend the foreign languages school two years before. They wanted to find out why I had been approached. According to the friend's daughter, after China was admitted to the United Nations in 1971 and Nixon visited in 1972, Chairman Mao had ordered a few select schools to start teaching English to students at an early age so that they could help China fight imperialism on the international stage. Chairman Mao was quoted as saying, "A foreign language is a type of revolutionary weapon in the struggle of life." How could a foreign language be a weapon? I asked Father and he said, "If you want to defeat the enemy, you have to know them and speak their language. This is an ancient military strategy." It meant nothing to me then. All I knew was that it was a tremendous honor because the program was established under the instructions of Chairman Mao and my parents were excited.

When the application form was handed out before the interview, I confidently wrote on the line that asked about family background: "Working class. Father is a Party member." We were told that the interview would be a way to gauge our political thinking and determine if we had any speech deficiencies. As we awaited my turn, I nervously rehearsed my answers. I was ready to parlay my family background and champion my own progressive record at school.

A soft-spoken man with thick glasses sat behind a desk in a small cozy office. He asked me about my family. I told him Grandma's story; how a poor woman, oppressed and exploited by the ruling class, begged her way to Xi'an to save her only surviving child. I mentioned that the child was my Father who, by the way, was a Party member. The examiner looked attentive and frequently nodded as I spoke. He said he was now going to say some words in English, and I should try to imitate him. "So-cial-ism," he said. It was the first word I ever heard spoken in English. It was thrilling. "So-cial-ism." I had said it thousands of times in Chinese, but in a foreign language it sounded exotic. I said the word. The examiner pronounced another word. "Re-vo-lu-tion." I repeated it back to him. When I came out, my older sister whispered, "You were in there a long time; that's a good sign." I said I talked about Grandma. My sister jokingly asked, "You didn't mention Grandma's coffin, did you?" I laughed and shook my head.

We were through the first round. Next was a medical examination for me and, for Father, an examination of his political background.

While I was waiting anxiously for news from the school, Mother vowed that she would not allow Grandma's coffin plan to ruin my future chances. Even Father agreed to put the coffin discussion on hold. Without understanding why her coffin had anything to do with my school admission and my sister's graduation, Grandma blamed Mother for turning the grandchildren against her. For days, she would not speak to any of us. I began to feel guilty that I was standing in the way of Grandma's dream of reuniting with her husband and thought of switching sides. When I told Mother, she pulled me aside. "Don't feel bad," she said. "You are still a child. There are many things you children don't understand. We can't allow a coffin in our house."

To "marshal" Grandma into complete submission, Mother brought her cousin over. The cousin, notorious for his loud voice, had just become a policeman through the connection of his father, who had been a driver at the Municipal Public Security Bureau. Dressed in a brand-new white uniform, which smelled of starch, he arrived on an old-style motorcycle. His presence at our house attracted gawkers, many of whom thought Father had perpetrated an illegal activity such as selling goods on the black market, a common reason for police visits in our area. "No crime is committed." Mother waved them off. "He's my relative."

The police cousin sat next to Grandma's bed, his fingers tapping in a teacup. Diplomacy was certainly not his forte. Without bothering to ask about Grandma's illness, he went right into the subject at hand.

"Huang Mama," he bellowed. "I heard that you want a coffin made. Why do you want to do that? You know it's risky, don't you?"

Grandma looked nervous. She cringed at the police cousin's loudness, but out of politeness, she listened attentively.

"You are not living in a village anymore," he continued. "Xi'an is a big city and all big cities in China have strict bans on burials. If you are not careful, you could get arrested." The cousin then told Grandma how his fellow policemen had been tipped off by neighbors that a man had purchased high-quality pinewood to prepare a coffin for his dying father. Police showed up, forcing the man to chop up the wood into pieces before detaining him for three days. His company also took disciplinary action against him. That was not the end of it, the police cousin said. Under the supervision of the street committee, the father's body was shipped directly to the crematorium.

The cousin then winked at Mother. I knew that he was exaggerating to intimidate Grandma. I could not keep a straight face. Father tried to shoo me away, but I refused to leave.

"Huang Mama, after you die, I can use my connections to help with your burial in Henan." The cousin tilted his upper body toward Grandma. "But don't rush and pester your son for a coffin now. If neighbors report you, not only will your son and grandson be in trouble, but also the street committee will intervene and make sure that we cremate you. If that happens, there is nothing I can do."

Before he left, the cousin played up my case. "They have stringent political requirements for your grandson's school," he warned. "Once he learns to speak a foreign language, he can be Chairman Mao's interpreter and he can be a big shot. You don't want to deprive him of this opportunity, do you?"

The police cousin wasn't always Mother's favorite. She used to complain he was too smug and disrespectful. However, Mother was certainly satisfied with her cousin's performance that day. At dinner that night, Grandma caved in. "My coffin can wait," she said. "I will keep myself alive until my grandson is admitted to the new school."

Thus, peace reigned in my family for the next four months, during which time our family attention was temporarily switched from Grandma's coffin to my sister's graduation. In June, my sister officially signed up to join thousands of high school graduates to settle in the countryside. As a Party member, Father openly supported her action, but privately he was deeply worried. According to Father's later accounts, he reasoned that Chairman Mao had used the fiery spirit of young people to get rid of his political opponents during the Cultural Revolution, but when his Red Guards continued to wreak havoc, he needed to restore stability. Moving them to the countryside would shift their energy and passion to something more constructive and alleviate urban congestion. Mother had heard about the neglect and hardship suffered by the students at the hands of rural leaders, and how the government canceled their city residential permits to prevent them from returning home. "The Party sings its promises like an opera aria," she said. "Once they get you out of the city, they don't care what happens to you."

Father was aware of my sister's intention of using her experience in the rural area to obtain a college education. Without proper connections, he felt it was a long shot. "Each year, universities only recruit a few students from the countryside," Father said. "There is no entrance examination. Your fate will be in the hands of local Party officials. What makes you think they'll choose you? Those good opportunities will be snatched up by children whose families have political connections. Be realistic!"

My sister didn't see it that way and she insisted on going. It so happened that our family met the criteria for a hardship waiver—Grandma was old, my siblings were young, and the family needed her help. Only a limited number of waivers were granted, but Father's Party membership gave him priority. Mother had been actively looking for friends to help us. My sister was furious, accusing my parents of staining her political record and dashing her dreams. She had her teacher come to the house, but my parents stood firm. My sister ended up with a job at a state-owned textile factory, while many of her former classmates lived a nightmare in the countryside and petitioned the city to let them come home. None of her classmates was given the opportunity to attend college. My sister eventually saw my parents' wisdom.

I was luckier than my sister. In July, as my parents were about to give up hope, thinking that the opportunity had been given away to people with connections, the letter announcing my acceptance at the Xi'an Foreign Languages School arrived at my school and was delivered by the principal. It was a boarding school. I would be allowed to go home on Saturday afternoon but had to be back on Sunday evening.

My parents were happy to let me go. Father's niece often bragged about how her son, a well-known basketball player in his junior high school, had been picked by the state to attend a special athletic school. The state provided food and clothing and rigorous training so he could someday join the national team and compete on behalf of China in international tournaments. Father now had obtained equal bragging rights, even though my parents had to allocate twelve yuan a month, one-seventh of the total family income, for room and board. Grandma was sad. Father explained that I was going to an elite school to study in a program established by Chairman Mao. She wasn't impressed. "When I die, my grandson won't be here with me." She wept. Father said, "It's not like he's going away for a long time. He's coming back every weekend. If anything happens to you, I'm sure his school will let him come." Grandma looked forlorn and lost. Despite her illness, she helped Mother make a quilt and mattress for me to take to school. She also had me take her prized bamboo suitcase. When I left on the back of Father's bicycle, I was too excited to see her tears.

5.

PREPARATION

On Saturday afternoon, when Father rode his bike to my new school to take me home for the weekend, he told me Grandma's illness had worsened and the doctors had said that she might not survive this time.

The news struck me hard. I slipped off the bike, struggled free from his grasp, and ran to the side of the road to cry.

It was a miserable weekend—Grandma turned feverish, and she was in and out of consciousness. Dr. Gao prescribed more antibiotics and Dr. Xu wrote another long list of herbs for me to pick up at the store. Thanks to Mother, whom Father sarcastically called the "community radio," news of Grandma's deteriorating condition was quickly broadcast to our neighbors and friends, many of whom stopped by our house to offer help and suggestions. Not surprisingly, Mrs. Zhang and several of the elderly women brought up the coffin issue again.

"Don't just start looking for the bathroom when your bladder is bursting." Mrs. Zhang used a Chinese slang expression to illustrate her point that Father should start preparing for a coffin now. She warned that the government ban on burial made it impossible to buy one at the last minute and, even if one could find a village-made coffin, the price would be high, the wood cheap, and the workmanship shoddy. "They use this type of thin wood," she said, tapping on our front door. There was not just the coffin to think about, she said. "I heard you want to take your mother to Henan. You know those rural folks, they think every city person is dripping with money." She smacked her lips. "If you have to depend on them to help you, they'll charge you a bundle."

Mother nodded vigorously. "You are absolutely right. Every one of our relatives in Henan thinks we are better off than they are, and they use every excuse to ask for money."

Encouraged by Mother's comments, Mrs. Zhang told Father to pick pine or cypress, the traditional woods for coffins. "I heard you can get them really cheap in a black market at the foot of the Qinling Mountains outside Xi'an," she whispered.

I had never seen Father engage in long conversations with Mrs. Zhang. He even offered her a cup of tea and probed her for details—the style of coffin to choose and what ceremonial customs to follow.

Now that my sister and I were firmly on the right path, Mother had no legitimate excuse to thwart Grandma's plan. She dropped her earlier opposition and urged Father to act fast. I guess Grandma's seemingly imminent death and the fear of retribution for not fulfilling a dying person's wish had changed her attitude. In addition, if having a coffin made in Xi'an could save us money, she could not let that good opportunity pass us by.

Instead of tending to Grandma's illness, my parents became preoccupied with her coffin. As usual, Mother left for her aunt's place in the southern section of town to borrow money. Father went back to his close friend, Li, who headed the city's Light Industry Bureau, and sought advice. Li called the Party secretary at Father's company, asking him to grant Father an exception. "Your Party secretary will turn a blind eye to your situation, as long as nobody files a complaint against you. Otherwise, he would be obligated to investigate," Li said. "So, tell your wife to keep it quiet."

By Sunday evening, when it was time to return to school, I begged Father to write my teacher a note so I could take a week off and help. He shook his head emphatically. "There isn't much you can do now," he said. "You are the eldest grandson and you have a bigger role to play later."

While I was away at school, my parents were busy enlisting relatives and coworkers for their clandestine coffin operation. Mother's aunt lent our family one hundred yuan to purchase wood—our family of seven lived on a combined income of eighty-five yuan a month, and it took Father three years to pay off the loan. A relative who worked for the Provincial Transportation Department had one of the drivers whose route took him past the Qinling Mountains outside Xi'an look for cypress

or pine, and he secured a load of pine planks; he even negoti-
ated a substantial discount. Several curious neighbors nodded at
Father's explanation that the thick planks in our courtyard were
for furniture he was making for the house. They admired the tim-
ber and asked, casually, after Grandma's health.

Finding a carpenter was more difficult. The father of a classmate of mine, Feng, headed the carpentry team at Father's company. He had been reported to the boss for taking several days off,
claiming to be ill, so he and a coworker could make furniture and
coffins in the rural areas in neighboring Gansu Province for extra
cash. Feng's father was detained and brought before a condemnation meeting attended by all the company's employees and their
families who raised their fists and shouted: "Down with capitalist
greed." Feng stayed away from school for several weeks.

Father asked his friends if they knew of a carpenter, but no one
could help. He was on the verge of despair when a laborer he had
once befriended came to the rescue. He had heard of Grandma's
situation and volunteered his carpentry skills. He promised to
bring two other Henan friends and, if Mother would serve them
good liquor and food, they would do the job for free so no one
could accuse them of moonlighting.

Mrs. Zhang studied the lunar calendar and chose an auspicious
date for the carpenters to start the job. Father thanked her, but,
sounding like a progressive, tradition-defying Communist Party
member, said, "We are urban folk and we live in a new society
now. We don't need to follow those rules." In truth, he and Mother
had already decided on the two-day National Day holiday when
the carpenters from Henan would conveniently "come for a visit."

At about eight o'clock on the morning of October 1, the carpenter and his two friends arrived. Mother pulled me and my sisters out of bed and sent us out to play, reminding us not to say a word. When we returned at lunchtime, the air smelled of pine and the yard was strewn with wood shavings and sawdust. Lunch was laid out on a small table in the living room. A bottle of Xifeng rice liquor—a coveted local brand—that Father had bought on the black market was placed next to a big bowl of steaming rice, around which was assembled a veritable feast of four meat and vegetable dishes. Rice and pork were rationed—a pound of pork and one pound of rice per adult per month. I was salivating at the sight and smell of so much food when Mother dragged me into the kitchen and gave me a piece of corn bread. She promised to let me have the leftovers if I behaved myself in front of the guests. I understood.

Feeding the carpenters so extravagantly drained our ration; it would be a long time before we next ate meat. The carpenters went home that evening and came back early the next morning. At the end of the second day, the wood shavings and sawdust having been cleared away, the courtyard held, perched on two wooden benches, a coffin that looked like a boat.

I climbed up onto a small stool and looked inside. "The coffin is big enough for two grandmas," I exclaimed. I asked Father why there was so much space for such a little person. He gave me a stern look. "Watch your mouth." The lead carpenter quietly explained the need for so much space. "Don't forget that your grandma will be wrapped in a quilt and layers of clothes," he said. "We don't want to squish her in too tightly."

The last task was to seal the wood, and Father produced a bucket filled with lumps of amberlike resin, which the carpenters melted in a big pot and applied to the inside of the coffin twice. "The pine resin will repel bugs or insects," the carpenter explained. "Give it a couple of layers of black paint on the outside and it will shine beautifully. It would look even nicer if you can find an artist to draw a couple of longevity birds, like a crane or a phoenix, on the side."

After giving it a final wipe, the carpenters and Father lifted the coffin and carried it inside. Our house was not large and I wondered where it would go. Grandma's bed occupied the only spare space in the living room and my sisters already overflowed their bedroom. That left only my parents' room, which was shared with my little brother and me. There was a space, next to the window, where I slept. Mutely, I watched as my little plank bed was taken apart and replaced with the coffin. It became clear to me that I would be sleeping next to it.

"Are you going to be scared at night?" I remember the carpenter asking with a comradely tap of his finger to my nose. Father pulled me over, his hands fondling my hair. "It's your grandma's future home. What's to be afraid of? You are the eldest grandson, the coffin keeper."

I had been a coffin keeper for sixteen months and I still remember that first night when it loomed large next to my bed. The idea of death, which had hardly existed in my consciousness, suddenly took on a physical shape in my imagination. My mind would be racing; try as I might to think of something else, my thoughts kept returning to Grandma—dead. I witnessed the burial of an old lady in a village outside our residential complex one night. As her relatives wailed like we only heard in the movies, we snuck into the room where the old woman lay in an open casket. With a shaking hand and urged on by my friends, I opened the veil and poked my finger gently into her pale, cold cheek. My friends jumped back, which startled me more than the strangely waxen feeling of her soft skin. She was dead. Later, I told Father about it. "Stay away from funerals and wakes," he warned. "The spirit of the dead can easily attach to the bodies of children. You might be sick or have nightmares." I didn't become sick. Nor did I have nightmares about it. I even went to see the old lady's funeral three days later. The grandson walked at the front of the procession, carrying a bamboo pole with a long strip of white paper tied to it. I didn't understand what was written on the paper, but an adult told me the characters were about hopes for a peaceful trip to the other world and a successful reincarnation. If I had to bear that pole at Grandma's funeral, my teacher would probably never allow me to lead the Little Red Guards.

I tossed and turned in my new little bed, tortured by the knowledge that Grandma would one day lie in that box, as lifeless, pale, and cold as the old lady in the village. She would be gone and nobody would ever be able to see her again. I was shivering even though the night was warm.

What would happen to Grandma after she died? What happened to all of us when we died? Grandma used to tell me stories about how the spirit of a dead person would come back and begin life all over again, as a new person or, if that person were lazy and didn't help with house chores, as a pig. I didn't want to be a pig. When I asked my teacher about it, she said it was pure superstition and good children of the Party did not believe such things. When people died, that was it, nothing more, and their bodies would become like a cup of water poured onto parched ground, gone without a trace.

I must have dozed a little because I was woken by Mother's loud snoring and heard our neighbors, whose house shared a common wall with ours, come back in from their tiny courtyard, still bantering and laughing. Then the night was eerily quiet, and a fall breeze stirred the thick leaves of the fig tree. I was wide-awake. I remembered a story about a young woman who choked on a piece of food, and her family buried her and everyone was very sad. Three days later, a grave robber dug up her coffin in search of valuables, but when he lifted the lid and tossed the body aside, the food caught in her throat popped out, and she gasped, opened her eyes, and sat up. The thief screamed and ran away and swore he would steal only from the living. What if we buried Grandma and she came back to life? She would never be able to lift the heavy lid. How would she ever get out? I got up and went to the living room and snuggled next to Grandma in her bed. Sleep came easily.

As a "Little Red Guard," I was supposed to defend and fight for Chairman Mao's revolution, not to guard Grandma's coffin. Each time I looked at the Little Red Guard scarf that I wore around my neck at school, I felt a pang of guilt. I was even hit with a fleeting thought of reporting it to my teacher. Then, the idea of seeing Father being paraded publicly deterred me. Besides, Grandma could die of a broken heart and nobody would take care of me.

6.

DISCIPLINE

As her eldest grandson and coffin keeper, I represented to Grandma the reward for her sacrifice, and her supreme accomplishment—the Huang family name had carried on to another generation. When relatives or friends came to visit, Grandma would drag me to her side and she would say, "I can now die in peace." It was as if my two sisters and younger brother, who would often be standing next to me, did not exist. Grandma doted on my elder sister, the firstborn, but she was a girl and "Girls are like water poured out of a pitcher into someone else's cup." She would marry and join her husband's family. My elder sister would say Grandma was "being feudalistic" and as she and my other sister went off in a huff, Grandma would shake a finger at their backs and say, "If they act like this, no men will want to marry them." My younger brother believed Grandma treated him as little more than my sidekick, and even now, whenever family is concerned, he remembers this. "Why don't you step up?" he says. "After all, you are the oldest son and the important one."

My parents reproached Grandma for her open display of favoritism, but they were guilty of the same adherence to Confucian filial hierarchy, where the eldest son outranks any number of daughters who might have been born before him. When the father dies, the eldest son takes charge of the family and its obligations. For Grandma, it was entirely selfish. "If a family has no son, its name ends, and with nobody to tend the ancestral graves and honor their memory, their ghosts will wander forever homeless."

I was born in 1964, the Year of the Dragon, a traditionally lucky year for having babies. More important, it was the year when the country was recovering from widespread famine; with food no longer a major problem, there was a surge in the birthrate. When the nurse brought me to Father, who had waited almost a whole day for news from the delivery room, he didn't know what to do. The nurse joked. "Check his toes; make sure he isn't missing one." He didn't get it, but nonetheless he carefully counted my toes and, satisfied they were all there, dashed home to tell Grandma, who was elated and distributed red-dyed boiled eggs to neighbors and relatives as tokens of celebration.

Mother was kept wrapped in winter clothing and not permitted to leave the house for a month, even though it was June. It is still a common practice in China, the belief being that after childbirth a woman should not stress her body with household chores or touch cold water because she is more susceptible to drafts and her pores are open to bacteria. If she contracted any illness during that period, the illness would stay with the woman her entire life. Mother blamed Grandma for many of her later ailments. Grandma burned her feet with boiling water in the first week and became bedridden. Father, who had never cooked in his life, was helpless. Mother had no choice but to abandon her recovery and resume her stressful household duties.

My first test was *man yue*, when a child is officially presented to a big gathering of family and friends thirty days after the birth. At my *man yue*, Father fussed over the name, which Chinese believe determines a person's future. So Father turned to a highly educated old man in our neighborhood who knew the basics of numerology and, after two days of complicated calculations based on the exact time and place of my birth, he came up with two characters, "Wen" and "Guang," which mean "culturally wide." I would be a scholar. Father knew the teachings of Confucius: "Those who work with their brains rule those who work with their hands." Wenguang was also the name of one of Father's heroes, the twelfth-century warrior-scholar who had fought barbarian invaders on China's northwestern borders. By choosing that name, Father was going against Communist convention. In the mid-1960s, many parents opted for more progressive names for their sons to express their loyalty to the Party: "Yaojin," to honor Chairman Mao's Great Leap Forward; or "Wenge," the Cultural Revolution; or "Weihong," "defending the Red Revolution."

My status as the eldest grandson meant the world to Grandma but not to Mother who, like many women of her generation, placed the Revolution above their families. Five weeks after I was born, Mother returned to work at a company that manufactured rubber tires and tubes. A member of the company's Young Women's Commando, a production team that had been recognized by the Party for their high productivity and their taking on equally challenging tasks as men, Mother put in long hours and only came home on the weekends. "There was a stigma against taking time off to care for your own children," Mother would explain years later about her absence in the early part of my life, citing the story of her team leader who missed her father's funeral because she would not allow his death to distract her from the revolutionary work.

Without Mother's presence, Grandma became my surrogate mother and kept me close to her, in much the same way she did with Father. Living space was at a premium and our family, like many city dwellers in China, occupied only two rooms, one of which was reserved for Grandma. I slept with her on a narrow plank bed. She fed me diluted cow's milk. When I became sick, which happened frequently, Grandma would carry me on her back and wobble her way to a nearby hospital.

When I was two and a half, my parents were shocked that I had problems talking. Father took me to a doctor, where he was reassured that I was just a late starter. Unconvinced, Grandma began pressuring my parents to have another child, hoping it would be a boy. This was before the government implemented the one-child policy. In those days, Chairman Mao encouraged mothers to give birth to more children, believing that a large population would boost China's ability to triumph in wars against our enemies in the West. My parents obliged, but to Grandma's disappointment, the next child was a girl. When I was four, I finally got a younger brother.

Even though my new sister and brother went with Mother to be looked after by her company's child-care unit, Grandma kept me at home, arguing that the welfare of the eldest grandson was critical to the Huang family and could not be left to the responsibility of strangers. Grandma would share her food with me and kept a stockpile of fruit and cakes brought by visitors in a small bamboo suitcase next to her pillow. She would sneak me a snack from time to time. Such treats were not to be shared with my siblings.

My well-being seemed to be the concern of many elderly Huang relatives. I recall visiting a grandaunt in a village outside Xi'an. She was alarmed by my anemic appearance, reprimanded Father for not taking better care of me, and sent us a goat so that I could have fresh milk every day. Grandma milked the goat every morning and filled two big bowls. In our crowded tenement, the goat caused much trouble for Father, who reasoned that I should be responsible for it since it was for my benefit. During summer breaks, I'd take the goat to the field outside our residential complex every day. The neighborhood took to calling me the "urban shepherd boy."

Grandma's doting on me as if I were an only child turned me into something of a brat with a streak of stubbornness. When Father didn't buy me a pair of shoes that I wanted on Lunar New Year, I yanked the cloth from the table already piled with food for the holiday celebrations, ruining days of work by Mother, who blamed Grandma for turning me into a "little tyrant."

I soon learned that being the eldest son was not all about adulation. It brought with it strict discipline. When Mother was in her mid-thirties, Father managed to transfer her to his company as an assembly-line supervisor, which meant that suddenly she was around more often. As the mother of four children, she lost her youthful passion about her "revolutionary work" at the factory. Instead, she realized she needed to be more involved in my upbringing and was determined to straighten me out and break Grandma's hold over my life, starting with my preschool education.

I had problems adjusting to the change. I felt no emotional attachment to my mother at that time. She was to me more a stern relative than an indulgent mother and I feared her, even when she tried to buy me over with snacks and treats. The bond I had with her was not the same as the one I had with Grandma, whom Mother came to blame for our alienation. Mother took to punishing me, as if by hurting me she was hurting Grandma. She would scold me if I made a mistake. If Grandma intervened, she would escalate to spanking.

One day, Mother had come home early from her morning shift at the company's foundry, her face smeared with lead dust. She told me to fetch a basin of warm water. My mind was deeply into a novel I was reading and, after I poured the hot water, I forgot to mix it with cold. Mother scalded her hands and rebuked me. I puckered my nose in defiance while her back was turned, but she caught me and, furious, slapped me across the face. Blood poured from my nose. Grandma jumped up from her corner bed in

protest, which only made things worse. Mother grabbed the strap
Father used to mete out discipline and began to beat me across the
back. I was crying now, clutching her leg, but she kept hitting me
so I bit her thigh. Stunned, her vehemence grew and she slapped
all the harder. Grandma managed to pull me away, yelling, "Do
you know how dangerous it is to hit his face?" Mother screamed
back at Grandma. "Did you see what this spoiled brat has done?
It's your fault!" Grandma ignored her and, hunched over me,
wiped the blood from my face and staunched my bleeding nose
while my sobbing became louder and more dramatic and I began
to twitch my arms and legs for added effect. Mother relented,
but when Father got in from work, she launched into a verbal
attack on Grandma, who remained silent until Mother calmed
down and went out on an errand. Then, Grandma began cursing
Mother for her reckless beating. Father was put in an impossible
position and could only offer a popular expression of the time:
"Spanking and scolding are expressions of a parent's love."

With spankings like that, my fear of Mother worsened. As a
child, I had for a while developed a stutter, which disappeared at
the age of five. However, when I was around Mother, my stutter-
ing came back. More embarrassing, I started to wet the bed, a
habit that drew constant scolding from Mother. I was often too
scared to get up in the morning, trying to dry up the wet spot
with my body heat, silently praying that Mother wouldn't notice
the stain. "The older you grow, the more useless you've become,"
she would yell at me. For a period of several months, my bed-
wetting happened so frequently that even Grandma became
annoyed and stopped shielding me from Mother's spankings.

Thinking of those spankings still triggers bitterness in me today, though Mother and I did manage to grow closer over the years. In those days, I hated her and secretly wished that Chairman Mao would send her far away from home so she would come home only once a year. In this way, she would miss me and thus treat me nicely. I vowed never to marry so I wouldn't have to put up with a woman like her.

Like many parents in the neighborhood, Father was also a firm believer in the effectiveness of corporal punishment. Spankings from Father were not frequent, but neither were they sparing. When he did it, he meant it. He used an elasticized strap with hooks at each end. Its original function was as a door closer to preserve heat in the winter. Father would keep a mental tally of my misdemeanors with the diligence of an accountant, and when he decided it was time to settle up, I would be taken into the inner bedroom and ordered to turn around and get ready for my punishment. If I resisted, he would seize me and push my head down on the bed. In the third grade, my test scores had slipped to the low nineties instead of the expected one hundreds and that was enough to tip the ledger against me. Father would unhook the strap from the door and tell me to follow him. I would begin to sob, hoping that Grandma would stop him. He would grab me and drag me into the room where my sisters slept and have Mother lock the door. I would wail as the strap came down on my buttocks, five, ten, twenty times. Grandma would bang on the door, begging Father to stop. When he was done, Father would say to her quietly, "You are spoiling him." Grandma told me: "Tell your dad you are wrong and will do better next time."

Father would be quite calm after punishments. If Mother was present, they would force me to kneel for at least an hour to reflect on my mistakes. Then, Father would recite the litany of transgressions since my last spanking: the theft of a small bottle of liquor from a drawer to pay off a bully at school; the destruction of two watermelons I had been sent to fetch on my bike, which I crashed into a ditch after trying to ride hands free; and so on. Mother would lecture me on how well behaved our neighbors' children were at home. I would nod and pretend to seek their forgiveness, though I just wanted to stand up and have it done with. One time, feeling particularly stubborn, I refused to admit wrongdoing and ended up kneeling on the cold floor for three hours.

My parents were proud of their methods. At a parent-teacher meeting, when my teacher praised me for scoring the highest in all subjects, Father, who had never coached me in my studies, responded, "He's not that smart; it's the result of good discipline."

Whether that was true or not, Father did instill in me a sense of responsibility for the family, constantly reminding me of my obligations to honor the family name. Having learned from his own life experience that one could only advance within the system of the Communist Party, Father strongly encouraged me to be active in politics.

For me, Communist indoctrination began early. When American preschoolers were reading Dr. Seuss or watching *Sesame Street*, we were memorizing Chairman Mao, starting with his simpler quotations and graduating to whole essays by elementary school. Thanks to visits to Mother's factory, my revolutionary vocabulary was extensive because I asked what this or that character meant until I could easily read banners—DOWN WITH THE COUNTERREVOLUTIONARIES AND RIGHTISTS and THE WORKING CLASS IS THE LEADER OF THE REVOLUTION. When I became the first to recite the three famous essays by Chairman Mao in first grade, I was made class leader.

Throughout my elementary and high school years, I was head of the Little Red Guards and the Communist Youth League. However, when I spent too much time in political activities, joining adults in promoting the Party's policies on the street, or spending days preparing the school's bulletin board, Father became worried. "Political opportunities pass like clouds," he advised. "The important thing is to learn a real skill, which will sustain and benefit you all your life."

At school, we were frequently asked our plans for the future. The correct answer was: "Follow Chairman Mao's words and be a qualified successor to the Revolution." We all assumed that a "qualified successor to the Revolution" meant helping poor peasants in the remote desert or mountainous regions. In 1975, the Communist Party was promoting a model student who turned in a blank sheet of paper during an exam, claiming that he was too busy with the Revolution to prepare for his tests. The whole nation was urged to reform the education system, which the Party believed was out of touch with the lives of workers and peasants. At school, we were encouraged to spend less time on our science lessons and more time doing physical labor, such as collecting horse manure on the street or helping peasants pull weeds. Father was deeply troubled by this new political trend and, though he made no protest about what happened at school, he forced us to read our books at home to make up for the time wasted in class. "This country is out of whack," he said to Mother and, noticing I had heard him, said, "Don't repeat what I just said to your teacher. Keep up with your studies."

Many times he reminded me how his future was stunted by his lack of an academic degree. "I was illiterate until the age of twenty and taught myself how to read and write," he lamented. He believed that if he had attended senior high or college, life would have been different, even though Mother pointed out with her usual sarcasm that "If you had gone to college, you would have been labeled a bourgeois and locked up in a cowshed somewhere."

Father's favorite phrase in those days was "The water flows downhill and people climb uphill." He would say, "No matter who is in power, sooner or later they'll need the well educated to rule the country." He required me to score high in every subject. He had Mother send gifts, such as extra coupons for oil and sugar, to my head teacher, who assigned me extra readings.

Despite Father's insistence that we should do well in our schoolwork, he also realized that we were facing a grim future, especially before I entered the boarding school. If the political policy remained unchanged, my younger sister and I would have to be sent to the countryside after graduating from high school. Each family was only allowed to keep one child in the city, and my elder sister had used up our quota. So, he began encouraging me and my younger sister to learn special skills that would help us survive the harsh working conditions if we were to settle in the rural areas.

Father had me practice my calligraphy and drawing for hours on end because he believed every village would need calligraphers to copy letters for officials, write posters, or design outdoor bulletin boards. He also had me take acupuncture lessons from Dr. Xu so I could be a barefoot doctor, a farmer who had basic medical and paramedical training at a rural clinic. For my sister, he forced her to learn to play the *erhu*, a two-stringed violin, hoping that she could join an army or village performance troupe. When she showed neither interest nor talent, Father had Grandma teach her how to cook so she could work in a rural communal kitchen, which was a relatively easy job and offered plenty to eat.

As a child, I was thin and weak and a constant target of bullies. This embarrassed Father, who had to escort me to school. "Why don't you fight back," he fumed after an older boy had beaten me up, leaving me with a bloody nose. So he took me to "Uncle Ren," who was a master of Chen-style tai chi and would teach me self-defense skills. "Your great-grandfather was both a scholar and a warrior at the imperial court," he reminded me. "I didn't have the opportunity to do martial arts. You need to carry on that tradition."

I was excited. Bruce Lee meant nothing to most mainland Chinese, but I had seen kung fu fighting and knew the fast moves and kicks would be useful in defending myself against the bullies at school. Father brought me to his house with gifts and he officially took me on as his student. Over the next five years, Uncle Ren would coach me twice a week but tai chi wasn't at all what I expected. I soon became bored with its slow movements. Uncle

Ren said that if I mastered the real essence, I could be an invincible fighter capable of combining both mental and physical power. All I wanted was to beat someone up. Father forced me to practice. I would lie on the floor and doze, jumping up to practice when I heard his approaching footsteps. I gave up when I started at my boarding school because only some old teachers practiced it in the morning and I felt too embarrassed to join their ranks. But by then, the practice had paid off, and I had become quite good at sports.

Often, the teachings I received at home contradicted what I was taught in school. For example, the most important lessons at home were about filial piety, the ultimate expression of which was to take care of Grandma. I was never allowed to disobey Grandma or my parents. In the evenings, when Grandma had to tread her way to the outdoor latrine two blocks away, I was the one to accompany her. During rainy days, she would use a chamber pot and I would clean it for her. When the neighbors noticed, many agreed with Father, commending me for being a filial child. For a while, the chamber pot became a badge of honor for me.

In my third year at elementary school, we were taught that filial piety was part of the old Confucian philosophy, which needed to be eliminated. "Only Chairman Mao and the Communist Party are your closest relatives," said our teacher. "If your parents or relatives engage in any counterrevolutionary activities, you should not hesitate in reporting them or publicly denouncing them. It is a true test of your revolutionary will."

When I shared with Father what we were being taught, he cautioned me about believing in propaganda. "People might talk that way in public," he said, "but only the stupid or the fanatic would betray the parents who raise and nurture them. If you betray your parents, you betray yourself and will lose all your friends. Think about it—if you cannot even treat your parents with respect and if you rat on them for political gain, how can you expect your friends to ever trust you?"

At school, we were taught not to show any mercy to our enemies—landlords and counterrevolutionaries. In our physical education class, we were trained to use a wooden bayonet while shouting, "Kill, kill, and kill." We were told to retaliate against our enemies with violence, an eye for eye. As a Party member, Father embraced this part of the Communist ideology in public, but he acted differently at home. He lectured me not to harbor any thoughts of harming others. When a friend of Mother's sought help with a divorce petition, I promised to draft it for her, but Father flew into a rage. He yelled at Mother. "Are you trying to ruin the future of our eldest son? Helping break up a family is not an auspicious thing to do." Then Father turned to me and said, "Remember, when you do harmful things, you lose the protection of your ancestors."

Breaking an entire country away from long-held traditions practically overnight is a complicated business, and nowhere was this more apparent to me than in the contradictions embodied by my father. I grew up amid such contradictions, a fusion of ideologies and faiths.

7.

EXPECTATION

Owning a camera in China in the 1970s was a rare luxury. Families paid big money on special occasions to have their pictures taken at a photographer's shop. My friend Qinqin owned a Seagull camera, a black oblong box with twin lenses and a viewfinder on the top. Grandma had seldom been photographed and, with Father's permission, I asked Qinqin to come over on a Sunday and take Grandma's and our picture. Everyone was ready by the time Qinqin walked in the door. Father had on the blue Mao jacket Mother had tailored for him for the Lunar New Year. Grandma sat in her wicker chair in the yard, dressed in a clean black corduroy shirt and new velvet hat. We children were in our New Year's best. At Qinqin's direction, we struck different poses, but Grandma was her focus and she kept up a stream of chatter to relax her while aiming from different angles. Grandma's face twitched slightly; she was nervous, perhaps a little frightened, but she enjoyed the attention and bravely faced the camera. As Qinqin rewound the film, she whispered to me, "Your Grandma must have been a very attractive woman when she was young; you can still tell from her eyes, her skin, and her face."

"Really?" I had never thought of Grandma in that way. In my memory she was always old. I turned to look at her, examining her face as if for the first time. Her eyes were watery and sad. "Grandma, were you pretty when you were young?" I asked with the bluntness of my age. She looked a little startled and then blushed and waved the back of her hand at me. "No. I am an ugly old woman." Father laughed and said to Qinqin, "Grandma was indeed very pretty and attracted many suitors before she married Grandpa."

The tale of the faithful widow came back to me. I wondered if younger Grandma had been tempted on a cold winter night when she was alone and her son had gone to sleep. Did she flirt with other men? I caught myself looking at Grandma's hands for signs that she might have considered severing a finger to suppress her desires and strengthen her resolve like that legendary widow. Her hands looked frail, but there were no missing fingers.

Not long after the photo session, Grandma told Father that she needed the right set of clothing if she was to face death and told Mother to find a tailor to make her *shou-yi*. In the 1970s, clothing was standard and unisex: gray, green, or blue Mao jacket and matching pants. Grandma wanted none of that. For her *shou-yi*, she wanted traditional dress, clothing we associated with movies that depicted the old pre-Communist days. "If I die in modern clothing, my husband and our ancestors won't be able to recognize me," she rationalized.

My older sister chided her and said, "Grandma is too bourgeois! She wants to look pretty to impress Grandpa."

Grandma blushed and, as she often did with my sister, who, like me, had a special place in Grandma's heart, told her to go away.

Her demand for death clothes surprised me. Father said that Grandma used to be very meticulous about her looks when she was young, but I remember her wearing only one outfit—a baggy blue shirt with plate buttons down the right side, an ugly pair of pantaloons, and white knee socks. Her gray hair was always combed into a tight bun at the back. I doubt she ever looked at herself in a mirror. I would often point out food stains on her shirt, and she would wave me off with the back of her hand and say, "I'm an old woman; I don't care." When my eldest sister fussed over clothes, Grandma would scold her for being vain. "It's bad for a girl to care more about her looks than her house chores. No one will want to marry you."

As she considered death, I suppose she was feeling the stirrings of hope that she would see her husband again and they would be reunited in a new cycle of life, for surely he too had been alone all this time. I think Grandma wanted to be ready for their special meeting, dressed nicely for her husband.

Mother, who had been a reluctant participant in our coffin

scheme, warmed to Grandma's request that she take charge of preparing her afterlife wardrobe. Mother lined up an army of friends to help. Frankly, I felt somewhat stunned by Mother's enthusiasm and I said so. "As a woman, I can understand your grandma's wish," Mother replied. "In our rural village, no matter how poor a woman was, she would dress nicely for two occasions, her wedding and her funeral."

Word of mouth led Mother to two women old enough to have seen and even worn those elegant old-style dresses of the 1930s and 1940s, and on their recommendation, she sought out a woman who was a recent arrival from Henan whose husband drove a rickshaw in Xi'an. Children in the neighborhood nicknamed her "Aunt Deaf" because she was hard of hearing. Aunt Deaf knew how to make the *shou-yi*, though Mother had to promise her husband that they would be discreet and that she wouldn't get into any trouble. She brought with her another elderly woman—"my assistant," she shouted rather unnecessarily. Mother prepared the women nice lunches and for three days they worked behind the closed door of my parents' bedroom. I could hear the clanking of the sewing machine, the snipping of scissors, and Aunt Deaf's shouted instructions to this woman or that. When I peeked through the window, I saw strips and pieces of blue, orange, and yellow fabric strewn about the bed and various women wearing an arm or a leg of something as others pinned and fussed.

While people always used even numbers for weddings, symbolizing happiness for the couple, Mother said funerals required odd numbers, so that death hit only one person. On the third afternoon, Grandma was presented with her three sets of *shou-yi*, one for summer, one for winter, and one for spring or fall. The centerpiece was a blue silk cheongsam-style dress trimmed with orange linen. Instead of embroidery, a yellow paper phoenix was glued on each side of the dress. Aunt Deaf held up a silk top and a cotton-padded winter coat of matching blues with paper birds on the front. There was a black hat with flowers and a pair of tiny handmade pointed shoes, even a knitted yellow quilt. All were held out for Grandma's scrutiny, who examined each item as it was presented, and then went through them again, more slowly, examining every detail. Grandma grabbed Aunt Deaf's hands and thanked her over and over, saying how lucky she was to be able to wear such beautiful clothes after her death. I did not tell her that I had seen traditional Chinese dresses in old movies and compared with them, Grandma's *shou-yi* looked fake, exaggerated, and spooky.

With her coffin and *shou-yi* properly stored away, Grandma was at ease and able to think of death as merely another part of life. For me, it was the beginning of a nightmare. I no longer invited friends home because I didn't want my teacher to find out what we supposedly good Communists had done. And I especially didn't want to give my classmates more ammunition for their arsenal of jokes about Grandma.

I did tell someone, but that was under duress. There was a boy with whom I used to play games after school. We started a contest to see who could hit a far-off target with a brick. Whoever lost would pay the winner ten fen. I lost, but all that was left from what Father had given me wasn't enough to settle the bet.

The boy threatened to go to Mother and demand full payment of my debt. I tried all sorts of tricks to get him to let me off, but he was too clever, so I offered to show him a coffin. We snuck into the house while Grandma was busy preparing dinner and crept into my parents' room. I removed the covering sheets with a dusty flourish and he looked at it, unimpressed. He told me to open it so he could see inside, but he was still unimpressed. I think he expected something scarier than the two sacks of flour Father had stored there. I was desperate and brought out the suitcase containing Grandma's neatly folded and carefully bundled *shou-yi*. He giggled and forced me to put them on. After I had put on the blouse, he laughed and yelled, "Your Grandma is a scary feudalistic ghost" and ran out of the house.

The *shou-yi* was scattered on my parents' bed, the coffin lid was half open, and when I tried to close it, I stepped on and rumpled the blue silk cheongsam. The folds were too complicated for me, so I rolled everything up and stuffed it back in the suitcase. Grandma found out and told my parents that night. Father was furious and the subsequent spanking was particularly painful. This time, Grandma didn't come to my rescue.

To my worries was added that of the boy's reporting me to our teacher. He never did, but he confirmed to a couple of other boys that my Grandma really was a freaky ghost and they stopped playing with me for a while, perhaps frightened by the fact that I slept next to a coffin.

Even though my parents reminded us again and again to keep quiet about Grandma's coffin and *shou-yi*, Mother set a poor example. The coffin and the beautiful set of shrouds at home became too much for her and she began to brag about our new family asset to her friends. Several came unannounced and were breathless with anticipation, as if they were about to see some rare artwork. Mother would urge them not to tell anyone, even though she was the one who was telling the whole neighborhood. Then she would bring out the little outfits and, as a bonus, uncover the shiny black coffin. Visitors would say, "What a filial son your husband is. Your mother-in-law is so fortunate to have you." Mother, long considered Grandma's nemesis, bathed in the compliments.

The casket and *shou-yi* were the most public, and riskiest, part of Father's preparations, and he managed those without detection. He was again elected a model Communist Party member, and at work he was diligent in his duties to the Party. At night, under the bare twenty-watt lightbulb hanging over the dinner table, he and Mother pressed forward with their arrangements, working through various scenarios, each with a litany of problems and solutions.

There were several potential plans for Grandma's burial, depending on the season in which she died, and Father drew up a list of problems and possible solutions for each. According to village custom, a person who has left and dies elsewhere becomes a wandering ghost and his or her body cannot be brought back for later burial. One solution was that, if she fell seriously ill, we could take her by train and bus and let her die in the village surrounded by relatives, who could also be enlisted in the plan. "What if Grandma lingers on for months?" Mother posited. "We wouldn't be able to take time off and stay there with her, would we?" The cost would also be prohibitive because, as everyone knew, Father lived in a big city, he would be expected to hold a big ceremony over several days. Father struck it out as an option and concentrated on what to do if she died in Xi'an.

If Grandma passed away in winter, early spring, or late fall, we would find someone who had access to a truck, the idea being to get Grandma's body to her home village as quickly and inconspicuously as possible. It was a twenty-hour drive over rutted, muddy roads. Father and I would accompany the body. We would set up a tent outside the village, invite surviving relatives for a simple wake, and bury Grandma in the family plot. Father's company had six or seven vehicles at its disposal and it might be possible to secure the use of one of them. If not, we could wrap the coffin and slip it onto a freight train. If there was no freight train that day, we would ditch the coffin, bundle up Grandma in a quilt, and board the next passenger train for Henan with a lie that she was gravely ill. By stuffing the quilt with ice, we figured we could make the six-hour trip without arousing suspicion, though there were strict laws against carrying corpses on passenger trains. We would need reliable friends working for the railway department because, if discovered, Grandma's body would be dumped at the next station for immediate cremation there and we would be punished and publicly condemned.

If Grandma died in summer, time would become a critical factor. If no means of transport could be immediately found, we would bury her outside Xi'an and wait for the third anniversary mourning ceremony to dig up her bones and take them to the village. This expensive and complicated option would involve two moves and much vigilance. A grandaunt, Grandma's cousin, who lived in a village a short distance from Xi'an, said she would have no problems finding a spot in her village cemetery until we were ready to make the proper move.

There was no question that what we were doing was illegal and anyone helping us would be guilty of a crime. Knowing the risks involved, my parents were careful in the friends and relatives they asked to help. Soon Father had compiled a list of "uncles" and "aunties" with all manner of connections and emphasized the importance of cultivating and maintaining close relations with them if it was to be a seamless operation.

8.

SECRETS

Mother always envied the close relationship between Father and Grandma. My maternal grandmother, or *po-po*, died when Mother was still a little girl in circumstances I can only describe as mysterious.

I had not given much thought to the fate of Po-po until Mother took me and my younger sister on a visit to her home village in September 1974. It was also in Henan, just seven kilometers from Father's village. Mother hadn't been home for fourteen years and she had planned the trip for a long time. It was a chance for us to meet her relatives, and an opportunity for Mother to become better acquainted with Father's kin, whose help would be needed for Grandma's burial.

Mother spent willfully in the month before the trip: new shoes, bolts of cloth for her sisters, jackets for her brothers. As the gifts piled up on top of Father's old desk, I overheard Grandma grumble to Father: "Why is she wasting our money on her family? They treated her so badly. Do you think her stepmother will even be happy to see her?"

Stepmother? This was news to me. Since we hardly had any contact with Mother's family, they were rarely discussed. I asked Mother about Po-po and her answer was terse: her own mother died and her father had remarried. Did your step *po-po* treat you nicely? "No," Mother said, and by her tone, I understood the subject to be closed. I felt a new sympathy for Mother.

Her father, my maternal grandpa, or *gong-gong*, met us at the train station. I had seen him once before when he stopped in Xi'an two years earlier. Mother looked just like her father; both had high cheekbones; big round eyes; flat, platelike faces; and loud, booming voices. Mother was crying when she saw Gong-gong at the station and they were soon conversing in what sounded to me like some obscure dialect.

After two hours on a long-distance bus and another hour riding a horse-drawn cart, we finally reached our destination. Gong-gong's house was big and dilapidated and had packed-clay walls. Step Po-po looked nothing like Grandma. She appeared to be only a few years older than Mother, though she wore the same blue baggy shirt with buttons down the side. Her feet were unbound and she was quite thin. Step Po-po greeted us in a soft voice I strained to hear, quite different from Gong-gong's howling. She patted my head gently. *This was the evil stepmother?* I said to myself. She brought me a small bowl of water. Tired and thirsty, I took a big gulp, but the water tasted strange and bitter, as if poisoned. I grimaced. Po-po giggled and everyone else laughed. Water from the village wells had been polluted for years. People simply had gotten adjusted

The next day, when Gong-gong took Mother to see Father's birthplace, we followed an uncle, and outside a tiny grocery, met an elderly woman, who was in her seventies. She touched my sister's face, saying she took after Mother. I sat next to her while our uncle ran some errands. "I used to be your neighbor for many years," the old woman said. "Your mother had a hard life." I asked why and she seemed surprised at my ignorance. She looked around to make sure we couldn't be overheard and whispered, "They threw your *po-po* down a well and killed her. Then, your poor mother's sister was kidnapped. I wonder how she is. Your step Po-po didn't like your mother." My uncle came back and the old lady immediately switched topics and complimented me on how smart I was, though the bombshell she had dropped had left me deaf. Po-po, murdered? Was that why the water tasted so strange? Gong-gong was a strong and smart person; why couldn't he protect her? Why was my aunt kidnapped? Did they shove rags in her mouth to silence her, like they did in the movies? My imagination ran wild. I wanted to be with Mother, to ask her questions, but she was busy with her half sisters and half brothers.

None too soon, it was time for us to leave. At the station, as Mother lugged our bags, which bulged with gifts from her relatives, Gong-gong carried me and my sister onto the train first.

While we were waiting for Mother, I blurted out the question that had bothered me throughout the trip: "Did they throw my *po-po* in a well?" Gong-gong was stunned for a moment and then mumbled in a low voice that scared me. "Nonsense! Who told you that?" He glared at me before turning to help Mother hoist our bags onto the luggage rack and then walked off the train. Mother waved at him from the window, asking him to go without waiting for the train to leave. He nodded, but didn't move, except to wave. He didn't look at me.

As the train roared out of the station, I told Mother about the old lady. "Yes, many people say your *po-po* was thrown in a well," she said. Her voice was calm, detached, as if we were talking about the weather. "Was there water in the well or was it a dry well?" I asked. "I don't know," she said. "It was so long ago. I don't remember much." Then Mother said her sister was kidnapped while she was playing on the street one day and sold to a miner in Anhui Province. They married and had five children.

I wasn't satisfied with Mother's answer and later asked Father, who used a phrase that came up whenever he was reluctant to answer my question. "There are many things you don't understand. Mother will tell you more when you grow up."

I waited for fifteen years. Mother and my younger sister came to see me in Shanghai in December 1989 before I came to the United States. We spent a carefree week together. None of us knew how long I would be gone, but I wanted to get something settled in my mind and nervously brought up the subject of Po-po, though I didn't expect Mother to tell me anything I didn't already know. She surprised me with a story that sounded as if it had come straight from a gangster movie. For many years, Mother said she was loath to talk about her family because many of her relatives had strong ties with local underground societies.

My mother was born in 1938 into a family of land-owning farmers. Her grandfather was village chief and headed a secret martial-arts society. But in 1936, his clan became involved in a dispute with another underground society and, on a summer evening, he was stabbed to death near the village entrance. The murderer was never caught.

Her father, my *gong-gong*, was the only boy in the family. He had eight sisters who were each strong-willed and ran the household after their father's death. In 1932, at the age of fourteen, Gong-gong had been married to a girl from a nearby village. She was ten years older than he was, as was the custom; boys from well-to-do families married girls who could be both wife and maid to the rest of the family. Though many well-off families required that the feet of girls be bound, hers were not because she was needed to help in the fields. Po-po was as strong-willed as her sisters-in-law and had a fiery temper, which I could easily imagine given Mother's explosive tendencies. She had problems with Gong-gong's siblings from the start. The sisters disliked the way Gong-gong listened to his wife and not them. While irreverence for the husband's family was grounds for divorce, in rural areas the end of a marriage stigmatized both the woman's and the man's families. "Accidental death" was the usual way to deal with disobedient wives. They must have felt further emboldened by the fact that Po-po came from a poor family and there was little likelihood of serious consequences.

After eight years of marriage, Po-po had given birth to two girls and a boy. Mother was in the middle. When famine hit Henan Province in 1942, Gong-gong's family did not have the resources to survive and many succumbed to starvation. When Po-po disappeared, it was assumed she had gone home to visit her parents, but she never came back. The official version was that she had starved to death on her way home, though there was no body to prove this. Villagers said that Po-po had been abducted by strangers, tied up, and tossed into a well. That account of events was plausible, and suspicion fell on the sisters, who were said to have connections with a secret society and conspired to kill Po-po. One of Po-po's brothers showed up in the village threatening to avenge the death of his sister, but he was waylaid and beaten to death by unknown assailants, presumably gang members. In the absence of contrary evidence, death by starvation was accepted as Po-po's fate.

With no one to care for them, Mother and her two siblings suffered tremendously. When her younger brother died of starvation, Gong-gong and other members of the family left in search of food. They took Mother with them because she was an obedient child. But not her sister, who pestered them about Po-po's death. Soon her sister was lost. Gong-gong said human smugglers had snatched her away. Mother was now alone.

Gong-gong married a much younger woman from a wealthy family. Unlike Po-po, she was even-tempered and knew how to please her sisters-in-law. Over the years, she gave birth to six children—three boys and three girls. Mother was miserable. She did the work her stepmother would not and was seldom given anything new to wear. There grew a mutual dislike between them.

In 1953, Gong-gong begged a sister of his who had moved to Xi'an to take Mother and find her a husband. Mother was fifteen. She stayed with her aunt for three years until a matchmaker found a suitable young man who had migrated from the same region and lived with his widowed mother. After two meetings, they were married. The young man was my father.

Father recalls that he was to meet two girls on the same day, chosen by separate matchmakers, and he picked the one who had come from the same region as he had. He brought her to see Grandma, who approved of her big round face and big eyes, a traditional measure of beauty, and her strong bones meant she could do hard work and give birth to many children. On their second date, Father showed up at the house of Mother's aunt, bearing gifts—two sets of clothes for Mother—and proposed that they marry, which they did after the formal three-month engagement. The Communist government was still replacing China's currency and people in Xi'an paid for most important things in sacks of flour. Father generously offered fifteen sacks to compensate Gong-gong's sister for taking care of Mother. Thus, my parents were married in 1957 and my elder sister was born a year later. Finally Mother felt she had a family of her own.

When I asked if Mother believed the story that Po-po had been murdered, she acknowledged that it was highly possible. However, she did not want to dwell on the past. "The past was past and I wanted to let it go," she said.

However, I found it hard to let it go myself. For years, Po-po's death and the kidnapping of Mother's sister lingered at the edge of my thoughts. I even developed the habit of going out of my way to avoid wells. I found it strange that the murder theory floated around the family circle for more than thirty years, but no one asked for a criminal investigation. Occasionally, during my visits to Mother's relatives, I would press them with the question. They either ignored me or silenced me with the perfunctory response: "It was during the time of the famine and so many people died in the rural areas. Nobody really knows what happened."

The issue resurfaced in the summer of 1976, when Mother's sister, Aunt Xiuying, who had been kidnapped as a young girl, came to Xi'an for a visit.

At the train station, I recognized her right away. She had the same loud voice, round face, and high cheekbones as Mother. She was choked with tears when she saw Mother, and soon everyone was crying. She met Grandma and was shown the coffin and, between loud sobs, said, "If my mother were still alive, she would be your age. I wish I could give her a proper burial. We don't even know where her body is." No one knew what to say.

Over the next week, Aunt Xiuying left a trail of tears and unpleasant arguments with her close relatives in Xi'an. Seeing Grandma's coffin triggered painful memories, and she redoubled her efforts to find her mother's murderer. She confronted Gong-gong's sister, who had brought Mother to Xi'an. What was her role in Po-po's death? Gong-gong's sister was visibly shocked, but insisted Po-po had died of starvation and Aunt Xiuying was too stubborn to accept the facts. The visit ended badly and, once word of it got around, other relatives who might have known a thing or two about Po-po's death avoided her. Even Mother began to distance herself, urging her sister to be more diplomatic. I admired her stubbornness and fiery spirit. I wished Mother could have been a little more tenacious in finding out the truth, but Aunt Xiuying said Mother was only four years old when it happened, which was probably too young for her to have many memories of their mother.

Aunt Xiuying's visit rippled across Xi'an. After she left, we were all too busy with the living to worry about the dead.

Letters between Mother and her sister became fewer and more infrequent. When I was a freshman at a university in Shanghai, I saw that Aunt Xiuying's hometown was along the route of the twenty-seven-hour train journey from Xi'an. I wrote Mother for permission to visit her sister on my way back during the winter break. I was given reluctant approval. I hoped to somehow reconcile them.

Aunt Xiuying's second son picked me up at the train station with his tractor, and she was waiting outside her small apartment building when we wobbled up in the dark. Everything was covered in coal dust: the trees, the building façade, the stairs, and her skin. When I washed my face, the water turned black. Before I could even sit, the sobbing started. "You are all grown up. Your mother and I had a hard life. Our mother was tossed in a well when we were so young."

Her husband, the coal miner, stopped her. He was shy and when dinner started, he didn't come to the table. Instead, he sat in the dark corner, chain-smoked, accompanied with occasional coughing. His face was as wrinkled and dark as my aunt's.

That night, I asked Aunt Xiuying about her abduction. Between
sobs, she told me what she believed had happened.

She had just turned eight when Po-po disappeared. She
refused to accept the official version of Po-po's death and bom-
barded Gong-gong with questions. Her obstinacy alienated her
from all the adults in the family. She felt lonely and took to
playing alone outside the village. A distant relative whom she
called uncle came along while she was in a field and whispered
to her that he knew where her mother was. This uncle enticed
her away and handed her to a stranger, who gave Aunt Xiuying
a candy and put her on a horse-drawn cart. The stranger was
part of a human-smuggling ring, and Aunt Xiuying was taken
by train to Anhui Province. Each time she asked to go home, he
beat her into silence. The now-long-dead "uncle" was an opium
addict who owed money to a local opium dealer. Threatened
with losing a hand if he didn't pay up, he agreed to trap some
local girls for them. Aunt Xiuyin was first sold to a family as a
bride to a seven-year-old boy, and she cared for her "husband"
as a nanny would, feeding and bathing him, but a year later,
the boy dropped dead. The family attributed their son's death
to the marriage, called my aunt a man-killer, and sold her to
another family. Her new owner worked her all day and made
her sleep on the cold kitchen floor, beating her for every mistake. Then a neighboring couple promised to help her escape
her misery, which they did, only to betray her and sell her back
to the human smugglers. This was in 1948. Aunt Xiuying was
taken to the mining city of Huaibei, where there was a profitable market for brides because no girl would willingly marry a

soot-covered coal miner. She was bought by a man fifteen years her senior. He was my uncle.

My uncle hadn't had an easy life either. He lost both parents as a young boy and was raised by a relative who ran a small restaurant. In his teenage years, he became addicted to gambling and constantly stole money from his relative. Unable to break his addiction, and having stolen from his relative and lost again, he was too ashamed to go home, so he went to Huaibei and signed up to dig coal. He was thirty-one when he bought and married my aunt, who was just sixteen. My aunt said her new husband treated her generously and, once they grew to trust each other, he gave her his wages to manage. He could become abusive after a couple of drinks, but after her years of virtual slavery, Aunt Xiuying felt secure and could tolerate his "bad temper tantrums." After the Communist victory, the Party made sure abducted women were free to leave if they wanted to, and my aunt said she thought about it. Though she had given birth to a son, she missed her home. With the help of a street soup vendor who recognized her accent as that from his own town and had heard about the murder of her grandfather, she managed to track down Gong-gong.

Aunt Xiuying returned home only to find that reality was quite different from her imaginings. She had problems accepting her stepmother and soon confirmed her childhood suspicions with whispering villagers too intimidated to speak out about what they had heard of Po-po's death. She confronted Gong-gong and his sisters, but was met with a wall of silence. She found herself an unwelcome guest; the home she imagined did not exist. She returned to her husband in Huaibei and gave him four more children. Gong-gong visited several times and they were able to rebuild a relationship of sorts, but she never forgot her mother. When I asked if she thought Gong-gong was responsible for Po-po's murder, she defended her father, just as Mother had done. "Our father was too young and weak. He was marshaled into the plot. He had no choice." However, Aunt Xiuying could not forgive Mother, seeing her silence as betrayal. "People who were involved in Po-po's death treated your mother very well, so she thinks the murderers are her closest family."

I had the strong impression that the biggest tragedy Aunt Xiuying had suffered was not the kidnapping and abuse, but the loss of her mother; she needed closure, which was what Grandma was also seeking by insisting on a proper funeral. "Like my mother, your grandma doesn't want to be alone anymore," my aunt said.

9.

RECOVERY

The coffin and *shou-yi* seemed to work against the evil spirits, or maybe it was Dr. Xu's herbal medicines; Grandma survived her illnesses and recovered. Unfortunately, she became too weak to cook for the whole family every day, but having dominated the kitchen for decades, she found it hard to give that up.

Most of my childhood memories about Grandma are associated with her cooking. While she reigned, she had her ritual. Since rice was a southern crop and not readily available in the north, Father loved noodles and buns, and Grandma cooked them almost every night, starting from scratch, from flour to dough to finely cut noodles and puffed-up steamed buns. Thus, we all became noodle aficionados. She didn't bring out the food or set the table until Father came home. She wouldn't budge even if Father's meetings kept him until very late and we were all hungry.

Grandma would never allow Father to enter the kitchen or touch the laundry. As a consequence, Father relied on her for everything. When Mother took over the kitchen, she inherited Grandma's ritual, always dishing out the first bowl of noodles or dumplings for Father and then Grandma. Unlike Grandma, who thought her son was irreproachable, Mother would constantly tease Father for his inability to prepare the simplest meal. Grandma hated seeing her son reprimanded by his wife. She complained to other women in the neighborhood about how badly Mother treated Father. My younger sister overheard Grandma's complaints and reported them to Mother, who became upset. Father would shake his head. "Two tigers cannot coexist on the same mountain! They will kill each other." Mother and Grandma were both born in tiger years of the Chinese calendar.

Grandma later saw Father's inability to cook as her biggest failure, and she didn't want me to be exposed to ridicule. Sometimes, before Mother came home in the afternoon, we would mix flour into dough and knead it to the right texture for noodles, cover the dough with a piece of wet cloth, and let it sit for fifteen minutes. Then we would use a rolling pin to make a big round sheet, which we folded and cut into either thin or wide noodles. I also learned to make steamed buns. A tough job in those days was to make corn more appetizing and appealing. About thirty percent of our food ration was corn. I was sick of eating corn bread and corn gruel. Eating corn was not only a necessity but also considered a proletariat duty. At my boarding school, we all pretended how much we loved it because it was the staple food for early revolutionaries. One day, at the cafeteria, I tossed into a garbage can a hard, cold corn bun. A classmate saw it. I had to write a self-criticism in my journal, confessing that I was under the influence of the bourgeois and had discarded the precious corn bread, made by the blood and sweat of revolutionary peasants. Grandma taught me how to make what she called "silver and golden" rolls, containing layers of wheat and corn. They were much easier to swallow. I used to tell Grandma: "When I grow up and earn lots of money, I'll never touch corn again." Nowadays, hardship food such as corn bread is coming back as a type of healthful food that is served only at high-end restaurants in China. I still avoid it at all cost. The mere thought of it gives me heartburn.

The only time that our whole family took a break from corn was during the Lunar New Year. Along with loud firecrackers came wheat and meat in abundance, even in those years of hardship. Preparations would begin eight days before the first new moon with an offering to the Kitchen God, who would report back to heaven. Grandma would first melt crystal sugar cubes in a pan and then fill a dozen triangular buns. She then placed the buns on top of a shelf in the kitchen because Father forbade Grandma to set up an altar for the Kitchen God. She said it was important to bribe the Kitchen God with sweet treats so his report would say only sweet things about the family, or at least make his mouth too sticky to say anything.

It seemed as if Grandma cooked nonstop for a week, emptying

an entire sack of wheat flour saved up over the year, mixing in water to make the dough for all sorts of wheat buns. Tradition had it that no one should enter the kitchen on the New Year so all the buns had to be prepared in advance: Round buns with a festive red dot on the top were plain; mouse-shaped buns contained minced pork and vegetables; and buns shaped like golden nuggets had red bean paste inside. Grandma and Mother boiled the red beans and mashed them with sugar into a paste. By New Year's Eve, Grandma had stockpiled more than two hundred buns, enough to feed the family and visiting relatives for a fortnight.

While Grandma cooked, Mother worked her sewing machine, which clanked late into the night, turning out four sets of new clothes for me and each of my siblings. All children had to wear new clothes on New Year's Day. In those days, the most popular style was a green jacket in imitation of a Communist soldier, with two front button-flap pockets and two small red rectangular badges on the pointed collars. I had this same style of outfit throughout my elementary and junior high school years. On the afternoon of New Year's Eve, the final touches on her sewing done, Mother would take over the cooking, preparing dumplings that would be served on New Year's Day morning and frying different shapes of wontons—"layered roses" and "flying kites"—for guests to eat with candies, watermelon seeds, and tea.

Today, people paste big red posters with messages such as *gong-xi-fa-cai* or MAY YOU PROSPER AND MAKE MORE MONEY IN THE COMING YEAR. In the 1970s, there would be big red posters put out on the neighborhood walls by the Party that urged people to CELEBRATE A SAFE AND REVOLUTIONARY NEW YEAR. The Party wanted to simplify traditions and urged people not to spend lavishly on food and liquor or gamble at cards, all of which were traits of the old society. Despite the Party's relentless campaign, they made slow progress with the New Year, which still retained many of its traditional trappings. The New Year was much anticipated by both children and adults. There were no red envelopes with freshly minted cash from adults, but it was the only time we had new clothes and could eat big white steamed wheat buns for a week. My parents never scolded us during New Year's, but we were forbidden to say anything inauspicious that could, Father said, ruin our luck for the whole year.

Even during New Year's, Grandma's funeral dominated our agenda. It was time to visit the uncles and aunties who would be part of the burial plan. The Lunar New Year of 1976 set everything in play. On New Year's morning, as the stream of Grandma's well-wishers thinned out, Father packed a stack of gift boxes of sweet cakes and put them on the back of his bicycle. Father might be frugal with us, but he was generous with gifts; being seen as stingy among friends was considered shameful. Often, he wouldn't allow us to eat the sweet cakes brought by others to our house and would instead rewrap them to give to someone else.

With the gifts all packed, Father lifted me in front of him and began our trip around the city to cultivate connections. First, we stopped by a certain Uncle Wu's house, located in a labyrinth of run-down huts and buildings in the eastern section of the city. Uncle Wu, who had been introduced to us by the daughter of Grandpa's first cousin, was the locomotive engineer who would transport Grandma on the train. After half an hour of chatting and updating him with news about Grandma, we each gave a box of festival cakes to Uncle Wu's mother. Our next destination was the apartment of an uncle whose mother was the aunt of Grandpa. That uncle managed a group of drivers at the Provincial Transportation Department. He had the truck and driver. I nicknamed him "Uncle Blinky" because he sweated a lot and blinked his eyes nonstop when he was nervous.

Our visits took until early evening. As I grew older, I wanted to spend the New Year with my friends and was a less and less willing participant in Father's visits; but he insisted that I accompany him as the eldest grandson. So began another of our rituals, the annual negotiation, which began with more warrior stories between visits and escalated into increases in my monthly pocket money.

His stories were the best treats of the Lunar New Year. Father, who struck people as taciturn and shy, was transformed at story time. He painted vivid word pictures, oftentimes drawing on old operas, movies, or books that had been banned. Before beginning a story, he would warn me: "Don't share them with others. Some are related to feudalistic themes. It could get your dad into trouble." Some stories, like this one, were clearly intended to reinforce what he had said about the benefits of Grandma's burial.

"An ancient general named Xue Rengui grew up poor. A local saint told him he should improve the *feng shui* of his family by moving the graves of his ancestors to a different location. He did and his fortune began to change. Soon Xue left home to join the army. Before departing, he did not know his wife was pregnant. His bravery soon gained him promotions. One day, a flood hit the imperial palace and many officials abandoned the emperor. Xue jumped into the flood and saved the emperor from drowning. Grateful for his heroic deeds, the emperor made him a general and he won many victories. Eighteen years later, he went home for a visit. As he neared his village, he spotted a tiger attacking a teenage boy. He aimed his arrow at the tiger, killing the animal, but also hurting the boy. Both the boy and the tiger fell into a deep ravine. When he arrived home, his wife said, 'Your son went out in the woods to meet you. Did you see him?'"

Before Father revealed the ending, he would ask me to guess. "Where do you think his son was?" He stopped his bicycle and wouldn't move again until I had the right answer.

"Did his son die after he had fallen into the ravine?" I asked eagerly.

"No, he survived because he had the blessings of his ancestors," Father said before we got back on the bike and rode to the house of Uncle Li, the Party official who was supposed to protect Father from any political fallout in case our burial plan ran into problems.

10.

ETHNICITY

In her relentless pursuit of a proper burial, Grandma was willing to convert to Islam and even change her ethnicity from Han Chinese, the single largest ethnic group in China, to Hui, a minority group that practices Islam. She had heard that there was a government mandate that exempted the Hui people from the burial ban out of respect for Islamic traditions. In her mind, the conversion could be done easily—as long as she gave up pork and started to eat lamb, the public security office would change her ethnic status on her city registration card and she would be spared cremation after death.

In the 1970s, there were about forty thousand Hui people in Xi'an—today there are about sixty thousand, among a population of eight million in the city. The Hui people were among the city's earliest residents and were descended mostly from Arab and Persian merchants and soldiers who had traveled the Silk Road since the seventh century when Xi'an was a prosperous cosmopolitan metropolis. Their Muslim traditions and customs survived down through the centuries, even though the Party banned all religious practices in the 1970s and some Hui Communist Party members were forced to eat pork to symbolize their break with "feudalistic and superstitious practices." Most Hui persisted in their faith and prayed secretly at home.

The majority of the Hui people lived in the western section of downtown and had created for themselves a labyrinth of traditional houses and mosques built in the Chinese architectural style. The mosques were closed during the Cultural Revolution and some were converted into schools or factories. But each time I visited the area, it was like stepping into a different world: The men wore white skullcaps and the women headscarves, and the restaurants were halal and the air smelled of roasting lamb. They make Xi'an's most famous dish—pita bread soaked in mutton soup, which was delicious and filling. The Hui people looked no different from me and my siblings, except their hair sometimes had a slightly brownish hue and some had blue eyes.

Before Grandma surprised us with her conversion request, my parents had also started to take a keen interest in the Muslim community, but for a different reason. They were searching for an alternative source of food to supplement our ration.

Though the Party propaganda machine constantly congratulated the country for its hard work in producing bountiful harvests, even into my adolescence food was always a problem for our family. No matter how Grandma and Mother tried to stretch our rations, they never lasted the month. During the summer wheat harvest, Mother would rise at dawn and walk out to the countryside in search of recently harvested fields where she would gather up any wheat ears missed by the peasants. Father would dry the wheat in the courtyard and take it to a nearby village mill to be ground into flour. I recall Mother returning home empty-handed after hours of scrabbling on her knees in the dirt. Some peasants had caught her in a field, accused her of stealing the food from their mouths, and confiscated the ears of corn she had found. At home, she cried tears of humiliation and vowed never to scavenge again for leftovers.

The lack of adequate wheat and corn worried my parents. During one of Father's consultations with Dr. Xu, he advised Father to introduce more protein into our diet. "They will eat less if you add some meat or lard to the food," he told Father. Since pork or chicken required ration coupons, Father traveled to the Hui quarters and visited the home of a Muslim colleague, whom we addressed as Uncle Liu, to ask if he could buy halal mutton, which didn't require coupons, at a discount.

A week after Father talked with his Hui coworker, he came in with the hindquarters of a sheep wrapped in linen slung over his shoulder. Grandma knitted her eyebrows, her face crumpled like paper, and she wrinkled her nose. "I can't eat that," she said. "The smell of mutton makes me sick." Mother let the mutton soak in water for a day before mixing it with two roughly chopped large white turnips and linen packages of star peppers with cloves and peppercorns in our large pot, and let it stew over a moderate fire. Father closed the windows and doors so the smell wouldn't make Grandma sick.

Mother served mutton soup with noodles every other night and I began to like it, especially after she added vinegar, cilantro, and some pickled green vegetables to enhance the color and flavor. Grandma cooked and ate separately.

One weekend, I was surprised to find Grandma heating up a pot of mutton soup in the kitchen, wearing a surgical mask. "I want to try the noodle soup too," she said, and at dinnertime she ate with the rest of us, trying to slurp down the noodles. Pleased that his mother had finally come around, Father said with his mouth full, "It's good for you in the wintertime." Mother was suspicious. She put down her chopsticks and questioned Grandma with a phrase popular in the movie world where a Communist would ask an enemy spy what his real motive was: "What kind of medicine are you hiding in the gourd?"

Grandma wouldn't look at Mother and instead addressed Father. "Jiu-er, do you have *guanxi* at the local public security bureau? Is there any way we can convert to Hui?" she asked. "We can offer them a gift if necessary." What did she mean? From where had this urge to follow Allah come? Father stopped eating. "Why do you want to be a Hui?" And the truth came out. A neighbor, Mrs. Liao, had dropped by that morning. Having lived near the Hui district, Mrs. Liao knew the government let the Hui people maintain a large cemetery and bury their dead according to custom for fear of offending them. When officials seized a small section of the cemetery for construction of a factory, the Hui demonstrated for days until the authorities abandoned the plan.

Grandma's conversion request shocked me because it was at the time when the racial tension between the Han and the Hui had escalated after a Hui person had hacked a Han policeman to death in the city's busiest shopping district. The mere mention of the Hui struck fear in the minds of many Han people. Ma Dasheng, a young Muslim in his early twenties, was hitching a ride and managed to stop a truck at a busy intersection in downtown Xi'an, close to the Hui section. As he was about to board the truck, a police officer intervened and forbade him from taking the ride. The two got into an argument. The official version has it that Ma ran over to a halal restaurant and came back with a kitchen knife and stabbed the policeman to death. Officials were outraged—it was the first time a policeman had been murdered since 1949.

Rule of law continues to be in its relative infancy in China, and back in 1975 the judicial system was barely functioning. The city was controlled by a Revolutionary Committee consisting of officials who had excelled during the Cultural Revolution. The committee didn't have to think too hard, and it gave Ma a public trial in front of ten thousand people and sentenced him to death. The Hui community staged a demonstration and petitioned the government to spare Ma's life because of his young age. The appeal for clemency was rejected. Rumor had it that the Muslims were plotting to abduct Ma if he was to be paraded around the city.

The day of Ma's execution was a Sunday. Thousands of people gathered to watch the parade, which was accompanied by the usual loudspeaker exhortations glorifying the "iron fists of the proletariat dictatorship." Father refused me permission to attend the parade and execution. He had also heard about the abduction plot and didn't want me to get in the middle of a riot. With the possibility of both defiance and risk, how could I resist? Public trials were popular entertainment and, on the excuse of visiting a classmate to borrow his notes, I joined my waiting friends and we headed into the city. I had never seen so many uniformed policemen. Dozens of military trucks with machine guns mounted on the roofs of their cabs passed by and groups of soldiers were scattered around the city. We had hoped to see Ma, but were told that his truck had already left for the execution ground. Apparently, he was wedged between two guards and his eyes were closed—he already looked dead. A rumor went around a week later that Ma had been killed before his execution to thwart any attempts to rescue him.

Murders are becoming more commonplace these days, and Xi'an has its fair share, but, overlooking the more extreme incidents of the Cultural Revolution, murder was virtually unheard of and the killing of a cop in broad daylight was terrifying. For months, Mother told me to stay away from the Hui section for fear of retaliation against the Han people.

We never told Grandma about the murder because Father told us to keep bad news from her. In the following week, Grandma kept pressing her case. "I know being a Hui person, you can't eat pork," she said. "That's not a problem. I can eat mutton. It will make me sick at first, but I can get used to the taste. I've put up with all sorts of hardships before and this is nothing." Father wasn't amused. "You can't change your ethnic status," he said. "And I don't think that eating lamb qualifies you as a Hui. I'll go to jail if the government finds out I lied about our ethnic status."

Grandma's ignorance was not unusual; many people then thought the only difference between Hui and Han was that Hui didn't touch pork, though none of us knew why, not Father, not even my teacher. I heard a story that Hui people, hounded and murdered by a non-Muslim ruler in Persia, fled their country. One day, a group of Hui people hid in a pig shed from soldiers who attempted to capture them. When their persecutors arrived and planned a search, the pigs dashed out to attack the soldiers and scared them away. Since then, Hui people have considered pigs sacred animals and refused to eat pork. While people in other cities called pork *zhu-rou*, or "pig meat," we referred to it as *da-rou* or "big meat" in Xi'an for fear that mentioning the word "pig" would offend the Hui people.

I only found out about the simple truth that Muslims consider pork to be unclean years later. Even now, ignorance about Islam persists; during one of my recent trips to Xi'an, people were still repeating the "sacred" hearsay about Muslims and pork. The lack of trust and communication had probably led to misunderstanding and conflicts in the first place.

Grandma's interest in becoming a Hui lasted only until she learned that the Hui people did not use coffins but instead were buried in shrouds. During a visit to our house, Father's Hui colleague elaborated that burial usually follows soon after death, and thus had to be nearby and without the complicated ceremony demanded by the Han. Grandma wanted a coffin, she wanted to be taken back to Henan, and she wanted the ceremony. The subject of becoming Hui was given its own quiet burial.

11.

DIVISION

Before the cold winter set in, Father decided it was still warm enough to add another layer of black paint to the coffin. After the paint dried, the coffin became a storage bin for the black-market bags of wheat and corn flour my parents bought as insurance against hunger. Layers of newspaper and two large tablecloths turned the coffin into just another bulky piece of furniture, and eventually we barely noticed it at all. Even though nobody made an issue of Grandma's coffin at work, Father never stopped worrying. He felt that Grandma's improved health only gave him additional time to save for the burial. On the fifteenth of every month, when Father received his monthly pay, he would add it to the pile of banknotes slowly accumulating in the locked top drawer of his old orange-colored desk.

Father's fixation aggravated the tension with Mother.

Growing up, every boy was subject to a ritual question from older women in the neighborhood. The question was supposed to test a boy's attitude toward his mother and future wife. "If your mother and your wife both fall into the water and are drowning, whom do you save first?" When my turn came, I said to a group of Mother's friends surrounding me at the home of a classmate, "I will certainly save my mother first. Who cares about the wife!" All the women burst out laughing. Then, when I added, "I want to be like my dad," there was an awkward silence.

Hypothetically, if Mother and Grandma were both drowning in water, there was no doubt in my mind that Father would get to Grandma first. All of Mother's friends knew it too. According to contemporary Chinese standards, Father was by no means a considerate husband. Never once did Father do anything that might be construed even remotely as romantic. My parents never just strolled together or took in a movie or went out for a nice meal, just the two of them. He had never bought Mother clothes or gifts during New Year's.

Even though divorce was almost unheard of in those days, it seemed for a while that Grandma's coffin was going to break up my parents' marriage. Matters came to a head when Mother was offered a work trip to Shanghai, which I knew was a place with many tall buildings and where they made White Rabbit candy. It was an honor to be selected and she would have the opportunity to meet city leaders during the trip. Mother wanted a new

winter coat so she wouldn't look shabby in front of the leadership. Father gave her the standard response: "We can't afford it
now. We have to pay off the coffin loan and then save money for
Grandma's funeral."

Mother exploded. We had heard them argue, but we'd
never seen them truly fight until that evening. My siblings and I
retreated to a corner as they had at each other. "I give you all my
pay each month, but everything you do is for your mother and
her coffin! You treat her like a goddess! Nobody else matters," she
yelled. Father went to close the door for fear that our neighbors
might hear, but Mother continued, her anger unabated. "It's sick-
ening. All you care about is your mother's death. Why can't your
mother be like everyone else and be cremated? If I had my way,
I'd burn the coffin so you can focus on your children and wife!"

With that threat, she stormed out of the house. Father sat
down, moping over tea. Grandma pursed her lips in outrage,
grunted through her teeth, and repeated a line that we children
had heard for years: "What a terrible woman. If she burns the coffin and has me cremated, my ghost will haunt her for the rest of
her life!" Father's fury was rekindled and he turned on Grandma
and, with raised voice, told her to stop such talk.

Having been brainwashed by Grandma, my elder sister and
I stood firmly on Father's side. I considered Mother's outburst
inconsiderate and her request for a new coat vain and bourgeois.
At school, our teacher encouraged students to live a simple life.
Wearing old clothes, especially jackets or pants with patches on
the elbows or knees, was seen as a badge of proletarian honor.
Mother supported the school policy. She had willingly mended

my shirt collar and patched holes on the back of my pants. Why would she make such a big fuss over her winter coat? Moreover, I resented her for threatening to burn Grandma's coffin.

When fights broke out in other households in the neighborhood, the wives would leave to stay with their own parents until the husbands relented. However, Mother had no family members in the city. She sought refuge in our neighbor's house.

Later that night, Mother did not come home. Father, too proud to go searching for Mother himself, sent me and my younger sister to check Mrs. Yang's house, Mother's usual hangout. "Your mother just left," explained Mrs. Yang's husband, an accountant at Father's company. When we returned home, I saw Mother and two of her friends, Mrs. Yang and Mrs. Fan, sitting with Father in another room, lecturing him about how to treat his wife nicely. "Funerals are for the living, not the dead," said Mrs. Fan, who had recently been widowed. "No matter how much you spend on your mother's funeral, she won't be able to see it. Don't be blindsided."

Throughout the evening, Mother's face remained expressionless. Father, an intensely private person, looked humiliated. My sister and I pulled Grandma outside so she wouldn't say anything that would stir up more animosity. "That's great. Now the whole neighborhood knows that your parents are having a fight." She shook her head and pouted. I held Grandma's hand to console her.

Mother and Father said nothing to each other for several days. Her face was clouded with displeasure. The house was quiet and very cold. My initial support for Father gradually diminished. I desperately wanted them to talk to each other. When, on the night before her departure, Mother came home with a new winter coat, all smiles and chatter, it was as if a dark storm had passed. Father probably realized he had gone too far. My siblings and I were relieved.

My parents used to share a bedroom. When my younger brother grew bigger, Father and Mother began sleeping in separate rooms—Father ended up sharing a bed with my brother while Mother slept with my sister. The arrangement, for practical reasons, was common in our neighborhood because sleeping space was tight for most families. I wondered if it was also Mother's way to punish Father.

Even after the coat incident, Father's devotion to Grandma's funeral arrangements remained unchanged. His penny-squeezing ways affected all of us. We all began shifting our positions, allying more and more with Mother against Father's frugality, which made us feel more deprived than other children in the neighborhood.

Before Grandma's coffin, my parents planned their spending with great care. Their combined salary meant we managed to get by comfortably. To the envy of many neighborhood children, my siblings and I would receive a tiny allowance occasionally to buy candies and books on International Children's Day on June 1 or buy a red-bean popsicle when the popsicle lady wheeled her cart to our residential complex in the hot summer afternoons.

Mother also had some money to indulge in her habit of hoarding. She was attuned to the cycle of shortages in Chairman Mao's planned economy, which ensured state-run stores got everything we might need, but never when it was actually needed. Nothing could be had, from sugar and vegetable oil to soap and cotton, without the appropriate government-issued coupon. Mother was acquainted with a woman who worked at a nearby grocery store and she would look the other way if Mother wanted to buy extra soap and a bolt of blue cloth with the right coupon. She would buy as much as she could carry and used her connection to trade for favors. When my favorite elementary school teacher ran out of vegetable oil, Mother sent her a bottle. Thanks to Mother, I was quite popular with several of my teachers.

Father could not fathom Mother's reasoning: enough soap for years, bolts of cloth bought in August to make school uniforms in January, enough cooking oil to drown the whole family. He never managed to control Mother's spending, despite having her hand over her salary on payday and locking it with his own wages in the desk drawer. When her friend at the store was transferred, Mother lost her connection, and Father couldn't resist: "Don't feel too sad. It's time you ran down your inventory."

In the post-coffin days, we all became victims of Father's belt-tightening measures. When my elementary school organized students to see a movie, I had to ask my teacher to write a note to Father, stating how important the movie was to my studies before he agreed to pay for my ticket. Before Coke and Sprite invaded China, we had *qi-shui*—a type of orange-flavored carbonated water in glass bottles, sold in state-run stores for ten fen a bottle. It was the most coveted summer drink among children. When we watched our neighbor's children take slow sips and burp loudly to show off their ability to enjoy the choice drink, we begged Father but he never gave in. Instead, he asked Grandma to pour cooled boiled water into a big white teapot every day, claiming it was a much better thirst quencher than what he called the "horrible-tasting" *qi-shui*, which he himself probably had never tried.

My elder sister was invited on a class outing at her high school, but Father only gave her a tiny allowance, half of what the other girls received. "This is for the future of our family," he said. "We need to save money for Grandma's funeral." My sister sobbed, repeating what our neighbors had been telling Father: "If you buy Grandma a piece of candy when she is alive, at least she can taste the sweetness now, not imagine what it might be like when she is gone." We were shocked by her outspokenness. Grandma intervened and Father grudgingly agreed to a small increase in my sister's allowance.

When I began taking violin lessons, my teacher said I had talent in music and urged me to undertake some professional training. I yearned for a violin of my own and found one in a store for only fifteen yuan. I pestered Father for months about it, but he would always say, "We need to save money for Grandma's funeral," and told me to borrow one from school. "I will buy you an expensive one when you become a famous violinist." He begrudged spending anything unless it was absolutely necessary or when, after one of my broken sport shoes flew off while I was doing a front flip during gymnastics practice and made everybody laugh, it was necessary to save face.

One day, threatened by bullies who demanded I buy them cigarettes and in desperate need of cash, I managed by pulling on

Father's padlocked drawer to open it a crack and, using tweezers, teased free a ten-yuan note. A week later, Father took out the leather strap and bent me over the bed.

Father looked for other ways to save money. Since meat and eggs were strictly rationed, he jumped at the idea of raising chickens in our courtyard. In early spring, Mother procured a dozen newly hatched chicks and Grandma fed them corn millet and kept them close to the stove until they were big enough, and the weather warm enough, for them to survive on their own. Father fenced off part of the courtyard, built a small corner coop, and let them loose. After that, eggs became a staple for different occasions. A boiled egg was my only birthday treat for years. Mother poached eggs in salty or sugared water when my oldest sister was in the hospital and needed protein; and Grandma beat a shredded egg in hot water mixed with honey and a dash of sesame oil when I suffered a sore throat.

Of course, all good things must come to an end. One of our neighbors who also raised chickens was caught selling eggs at a local black market. The authorities decided to ban animals in the residential complex to stem the capitalistic practices. One night, four security guards, trailed by a large crowd, headed for our courtyard. They chased after the chickens. Grandma, armed with her walking stick, hurled herself on one of the guards, screaming, "Leave those chickens alone. Kill me instead." She then snatched up a chicken and, holding it to her breast, sat on the ground, howling. It was all terribly pathetic. The security guards did not know what to do. Spectators began to cry. One guard mumbled, "Let's go. If this old woman dies on us, we have to take responsibility." And everyone left. I helped Grandma up and saw Father emerge from the house, shaking his head. "How do you expect me to face my coworkers?"

Relations between my parents remained tense for several years, but they reconciled in the winter of 1977 when, at the age of thirty-nine, Mother suddenly suffered severe internal bleeding. Due to massive loss of blood, her life was in danger and she required surgery. When a doctor explained to Father the risks of the procedure and had him sign a consent form, he said his hands were shaking. He realized for the first time that he could lose his wife. Mother's illness seemed to be a wake-up call for Father. When the company granted him a month off to take care of her, Father would leave home every morning on his bicycle, stop by a restaurant near the hospital to get Mother's favorite wonton soup, and then spend a whole day by Mother's bedside. I visited the hospital one day, and her roommate, a woman from a nearby suburb, raved about how attentive Father was.

Grandma was too weak to cook and my elder sister was away at work. With Father's lack of skill with chores, the house seemed paralyzed. I was eager to take on the responsibilities and show off my cooking. The lessons from Grandma paid off. I made noodles and steamed buns for Grandma and my younger siblings.

"I'm glad you can cook now," said Grandma, who didn't miss a single chance to criticize Mother, even though she was hospitalized. "In this way, you can eat anything you want without having to endure abuse from your future wife, like your father does."

Mother was still in the hospital during the Chinese New Year. In my memory, that was the first holiday that we didn't have new clothes. Our kitchen became eerily quiet and there were no steamed buns or deep-fried wontons. On New Year's Day morning, when the well-wishers streamed in to see Grandma, we had no snacks or candies to offer to our guests. Father said to us: "Now you all know what it is like to spend the holiday without your mother." We all knew that he also intended those words for himself.

The day she moved back home, Mother went directly into the kitchen and prepared Father a big bowl of noodles, just as Grandma would have done. I heard her talking to Mrs. Zhang, who popped in for a visit. "That old man in the house," she said, referring to Father. "He took care of me every day in the hospital. I now know that nobody is more reliable than your old man." My parents began to share a bedroom again.

In a morbid way, we children felt grateful for Mother's surgery, which had inadvertently transformed Mother into a gentler person. Notably, she spanked us less frequently. We used to joke that the doctor must have operated on Mother's brain too.

Meanwhile, we also noticed Father's changing attitude toward Mother. There was still no holding hands, kissing, or buying flowers, like married couples do in the West. Father expressed his appreciation for Mother in the typical way of a Chinese man. When my elder sister took a business trip to the city of Qingdao, known for its leather products, Father pulled her aside and told her to buy Mother a pair of leather shoes. But he never bought anything for her himself.

12.

MORTALITY

On a gloomy day in January 1976, China learned over breakfast that Premier Zhou Enlai was dead. By lunch, white paper flowers hung on the bare tree branches in the front gardens of my school. Funeral music, of the martial Communist kind, blared from loudspeakers. At lunchtime, teachers and seniors handed out black armbands in front of the cafeteria; everyone looked grim. In our English class, the teacher put aside the regular textbook and taught us two phrases: "Mourn the great revolutionary leader Zhou Enlai" and "Turn our grief into strength." I was only eleven and knew little about Zhou except that he was an important leader of the Revolution; it was hard to sustain sadness for the death of someone who meant nothing to me from a time I never knew.

Father was more concerned with the wider ramifications of Premier Zhou's death because Zhou was considered a leader in the reform of traditional practices and rituals. The official radio news said that he had left word with his wife that his body be cremated and his ashes scattered over "our vast motherland." Soon there were reports of a flood of requests for cremation and the scattering of ashes into the sea or on mountains. I wondered if Grandma would change her mind and perhaps want to have her ashes spread in the Yellow River—China's cradle of civilization—that flowed past her old village. I earnestly hoped she would, because I wanted to be able to brag to my classmates that Grandma was part of the river that nurtured us all. It seemed, at the time, to be a glorious end.

Father picked me up on Saturday and he had me take off my black armband and the white paper flower on my chest. "Grandma doesn't want to be reminded of death," he said. I knew that Father would use Zhou's cremation to try to talk Grandma out of being buried. Over dinner, he got quickly to the point about Premier Zhou's cremation. "Premier Zhou was a powerful person and he could do anything he wanted, but he chose cremation." Grandma was ready for him: "He was a progressive Party member and I am not; he did not have children and I have four grandchildren. I may be an old-fashioned ignorant woman, but I want my body to be buried so that my grandchildren will be blessed." Mother parried: "How do you expect your grandchildren to be blessed when their father is in big political trouble because of you?" But Grandma had heard that argument many times before and ignored it.

Over the next few months, Father lived on knife's edge. During my weekend visits, he would talk about how local authorities had started a new round of cracking down on burials, encouraging people to follow Zhou's example. Father told me later how he worried that local officials might come under pressure from above to uncover illegal burials and that they would force him to surrender the coffin. "I felt like we were thieves and had done something terribly wrong. Each time I walked into a meeting, I was convinced that someone had reported me to the Party secretary, who felt obligated to punish me." But the Party secretary never said anything, and nobody at my new school knew about Grandma's coffin.

It was the Year of the Dragon, supposedly lucky, but it turned into a year of calamity in China. My family had only a taste of it. On the night of August 16, as I dozed off while doing my homework, the lamp began to swing and the house started shaking. Mother grabbed me and my younger sister, and Father hoisted Grandma on his back, and we dashed out of the house. No one dared move after the first shock and we slept in the open. Our neighbors did the same. The next night it was raining heavily, and again the house shook. The epicenter of the quake was in neighboring Sichuan Province, in the sparsely populated area of Songpan, so the death toll was low. A similar quake had hit three weeks earlier and virtually wiped out Tangshan, a mining city not far from Beijing, but the government imposed a news blackout and we did not learn of it until well after the event.

During the day, the government radio used Chairman Mao's teaching that "Man will conquer nature" to urge calm and said the authorities were well equipped to handle natural disasters. When my parents were home in the evenings, they would share horror stories about families in Tangshan trapped under the rubble, waiting for help that never arrived because the hospitals had been damaged and many doctors had died. Humanitarian gestures from the West were looked upon with suspicion—Father said foreigners used the guise of helping out to infiltrate the country—and the government had refused international aid following the Tangshan earthquake. Mother would describe how thousands of bodies had been thrown into a big pit and buried right away for fear of an epidemic. She described them so vividly that it seemed as if she had been there. When my sister asked her to verify the sources, she would always attribute the stories to colleagues whose relatives or friends had been called to help with the rescue efforts in Tangshan.

Suddenly, the word "earthquake," which old people like Grandma had never heard before, entered our vocabulary and struck fear in our minds. When the earth shook violently that night, it became the most horrifying threat to us, more so than the evil Soviets who, we were taught, planned to attack China with atomic weapons. We slept in our clothes and were told that if we couldn't run, we should crawl under a bed or a table.

Interestingly enough, Grandma became more scared than we children were. With her bound feet, she wouldn't be able to run if the earthquake hit. She pleaded with Father not to give up on her. "I don't want to die alone," she said, choking up. She had

Father clean out the space under her bed so she could hide in there if there was no time to run out. Her expression of fear surprised me. I had always thought that Grandma was not afraid of death and was looking forward to reuniting with her deceased husband. Nonetheless, I was sympathetic to her vulnerability and vowed never to abandon her. Grandma was touched.

During the next few days, we experienced several aftershocks. No one had much faith in the ability of our houses to withstand a sizable seismic event, and there was nothing coming from the media or the leadership to suggest otherwise. Rumor and speculation were the only sources of news. The prevailing rumor at that time was that another major earthquake could hit Xi'an soon and that the government was withholding that information for fear of chaos. People began to take matters into their own hands. My neighbors took home sheets of plastic and wooden sticks from the factory and pitched tents in the open area in the middle of the residential complex. Several stubborn old folks, claiming that they had lived long enough and were not afraid to die, did not bother to move into the tents. An elderly lady even jokingly suggested that Grandma sleep in her coffin. "The lid is sturdy and it's quite safe in there," she said, "and if you get killed, you can close your eyes, knowing that all they have to do is bury you." Grandma was not amused. She told Father that she wanted to be where we were and did not mind living in the tent.

When the rainy season set in during the fall, the tent became dank and life was miserable. However, each time we considered dismantling the tent and moving back indoors, there would be a new rumor that another earthquake was imminent. The source was always a friend of a friend who knew a senior government official. The rumor was spurious at best, but no one was prepared to take the risk, to gamble with their lives. Father brought some concrete from work and added to the floor of our tent, built a more durable bamboo frame, and covered the tent with cornstalks that he had picked up in the field nearby.

In October, my boarding school made the unusual move of canceling classes for one month while other local schools continued uninterrupted. When my parents were away at work and my siblings at school, I was left alone at home with Grandma. Bored, I would sneak back into our empty house, lie on top of the coffin, and stare at the ceiling. The big wooden beams, which used to give me such a sense of sturdiness, appeared menacing. I lifted the heavy coffin lid, put it aside, and slid in, lying on sacks of wheat flour that Father had stored there. Feeling safe and comfortable, I carefully closed the lid over me. Inside, it was complete darkness. I could hardly breathe and darkness seemed to be swallowing me alive. I panicked, pushed the lid open with all my might, and jumped out. The coffin, to which I had become so accustomed over the past year, looked suffocating.

In the following week, I could not resist going back to our empty house even though the sight of the coffin had started to spook me. I was rummaging in Father's drawer and found a stack of books and Beijing opera magazines from the 1950s. The government regarded most Chinese and foreign books and operas published or performed before the Cultural Revolution as "poisonous weeds." Only those about the Communist Revolution were allowed. And here they were—magazines featuring stories and colorful pictures of those banned operas on full display. I flipped through some pages and became lost in my reading, absently sitting on a small bench next to Grandma's coffin. I realized that many of the stories that Father had told us were from those magazines. I began to understand why he loved traditional Beijing operas—each of which had extraordinary plots. The stories were completely different from what I had read before—the pulp propaganda about revolutionary heroes fighting class enemies. I was drawn in by those publications, which made me temporarily forget about the fear of earthquakes and death.

My favorite story was *The Wild Boar Forest*, an opera adapted from the Chinese classic *Outlaws of the Marsh*. It is set in the Song Dynasty and tells of a senior military officer who is framed by a corrupt prime minister and sent to a remote prison. The prime minister instructs the jailers escorting the officer to murder him when they get to the Wild Boar Forest. But a monk, whom the imprisoned officer had befriended on a visit to a temple and who had become his sworn brother, rescues him. The descriptions of how the monk ambushed the officer's jailers in the Wild Boar Forest have been etched in my memory.

"It was dark and deep, the most treacherous forest in the region. Many warriors lost their lives there. The officer hoped they would have it behind them before dusk, but the jailers deliberately dragged their feet. At noontime, one yawned and pretended to be sleepy. The jailers took out thick ropes and bound him tightly to a tree. Then, they revealed their true intent and pulled out their weapons. The officer begged for mercy, but to no avail. Helpless, he closed his eyes and prepared for his death. One jailer was about to raise his big thick wooden stick when a thunderous howling rose from among the trees. The jailer turned around and saw a big fat monk, who growled, 'I've been waiting here for hours.' The officer opened his eyes and saw it was his sworn brother the monk, and he marveled at how fast the monk's hands and feet were as he knocked the jailers to the ground. He was ready to slice off their heads with his knife when the officer asked him to stop. 'Spare their lives,' he said, and the monk sheathed his knife."

I must have been there for hours when Grandma found me. "It's dangerous to be here all by yourself," she said. Worrying that Father might lock his drawer, I pulled out some magazines and books, and hid them in the coffin before going out with Grandma. Over the next few weeks, when the opportunity presented itself, I would slip away from the tent, sit by the coffin, and read about warriors, emperors, and even a female ghost who refused to leave the world before avenging her murder. In a story called "Qin Qiong Sold His Horse," a warrior named Qin Qiong was marooned at an inn following a failed mission. When money ran out, he was forced to sell his favorite horse. At the market, he encountered another warrior, who generously offered Qin money to tide him over. The two became sworn brothers and joined the rebellion against the Sui Dynasty. They parted over different political views and ended up joining different military factions. One day, Qin learned that his army had set a trap for his friend. He tried to tip him off, but he arrived too late. His friend had been beheaded. Out of sadness, he buried his friend and built a temple so he would be remembered.

These stories conveyed messages that ran counter to what we

learned at school, that the Revolution was more important than friendship. I had learned a different set of values—friendship could transcend ideologies. Friends protected and made sacrifices for each other. I was so inspired by the warrior stories that I persuaded two close friends at school to become my sworn brothers. Like those ancient warriors, we planned a ritual where we would prick our wrists to draw a drop of blood, which would be put in a bowl of water that we would drink from. We would chant, "We were not born on the same day, but, if needed, we will die for each other and leave this world simultaneously." One boy's mother found out and notified Father. He was furious and asked how I had become so poisoned with those ideas. When he realized that I had read his magazines, he simply said, "Those are ancient stories. Nobody does that now." A week later, when I was home over the weekend, my sister said Father had burned all the books so I wouldn't get myself into more trouble.

As the books and magazines tempted me away from the real world, Father was moving in the opposite direction. The constant threat of earthquakes jolted him out of his obsession with Grandma's burial, forcing him to come to grips with reality. Before winter approached, Mother showed up at my school, where we slept inside a big tent pitched in the school playground. She had brought me a new winter jacket and a pair of underpants, and a pair of soccer shoes that I had asked for a long time ago. "Your father is worried that it might be cold sleeping outside," she said. "He took money out of Grandma's funeral fund and asked me to buy clothes for you and your siblings." I was overwhelmed by Father's unexpected generosity. I remember that all I could say was, "How is Grandma? I hope her coffin didn't get damaged." In fact, when Mother spotted a roof leak that dripped water onto the coffin lid, Father simply put a bucket there without fussing over it. He didn't even bother to paint a new layer over the damaged area after the leak was fixed.

By next summer, when the tents became unbearably hot in the day, people decided to let fate have its way and we all moved back indoors.

The earthquake was merely one tumult among many in 1976. On the afternoon of September 9, my head teacher burst into our classroom and interrupted our math class. "Please get yourself ready for some important news," she said. A few minutes later, a small loudspeaker above the blackboard crackled and broadcast a tune of mourning. Our hearts tightened. Chairman Mao was dead.

How was that possible? He was like an immortal to us. We had grown up shouting, "Long Live Chairman Mao." He was not like Grandma, who was fearful of dying unprepared. Even Father said he was different and would point at Mao's portrait on our living-room wall and explain how his physiognomy set him apart. "Look at his big forehead, such a sign of greatness. His face and eyes exude kindness. He's no ordinary person. He is heaven-sent."

All the girls in our classroom began wailing, as did our teacher. We boys didn't know what to do. But I was worried that people might think I didn't love Chairman Mao enough so I managed to squeeze out some tears. I began to think of Grandma. If Chairman Mao could drop dead like this, so could she, and if she died I would never see her again. My tears became real, my sobbing became a wail, and I passed out. The teachers were impressed by the depth of my grief over Chairman Mao. The school nurse diagnosed vitamin deficiency and gave me B1 and B6.

That day, we quietly went about our studies. Nobody dared laugh or joke. At home that weekend, Father said nothing about my black armband and white flowers. He and Mother both wore them too.

The deaths of Premier Zhou and Chairman Mao were national events and affected everyone. Wherever we went, there were portraits of Zhou and Mao, draped in black and surrounded by white paper wreaths. Big character posters went up wherever there was space for them, proclaiming THE SPIRIT OF CHAIRMAN MAO WILL STAY WITH US FOREVER; or ETERNAL GLORY TO THE GREAT LEADER AND TEACHER MAO ZEDONG. Looking back, it was ironic that Mao had spent his whole life preaching that humans were mortals and there was no spirit left after death only to have people like my parents want his spirit to be eternal. Every loud-speaker broadcast the same loop of mournful music and we took to humming along. Each class selected four students to stand around the altar set up at our school in four-hour shifts. Though I dreaded the thought of leading a mourning procession when Grandma died, I desperately wanted to be part of Mao's honor guard, which wore green Mao jackets and carried fake guns. In the four hours I stood at attention next to Chairman Mao's portrait, I thought of Grandma the whole time and what I would do at her funeral.

A week later, we were all gathered together in the school auditorium to hear the live radio broadcast of Chairman Mao's funeral in Beijing. My teacher stayed close to me, warning me several times not to be overcome with grief, and had a student watch me in case I fainted. When the mourning music resumed, my thoughts of Grandma returned and I began to cry, but so did everyone else. Father and other Party members at his company watched Chairman Mao's funeral on television. It was pouring rain in Beijing. "The Heavenly God is shedding tears for Chairman Mao," he said when we got home that night. "It always happened in the past when an emperor died."

Chairman Mao's death made me worry that Grandma might die soon. On my weekend visits, I got into the habit of using part of my allowance to buy her a packet of candies from a small store near my school. Meanwhile, Grandma's fear of death was intensified and she even started to regret having her coffin made, insisting that Father find a place outside our house so she did not have to be reminded of her own death every day. Father did not remove the coffin, but he covered it up nicely with old newspapers. He also advised us not to talk about Mao's or anyone's death at home. "Let's not stoke her fear," Father said.

When the nation was done mourning and had moved on, the Party decided that Mao's corpse should be embalmed and put on show, like Lenin's in Moscow. Father still had to figure out what to do next about Grandma's funeral, despite her newly acquired aversion to death, which Father interpreted as a sign of pending demise. He set about trying to locate Grandpa's grave. Grandma remembered only that it was on the tip of a small bend in the Yellow River near their village. Given that Grandma's village had been moved many times over the decades, Father had set himself a challenging task. A few weeks after Chairman Mao's death, Father hitched a ride with a company truck headed for Henan. He lied to Grandma that he would be on a business trip, but he had secretly stuffed his bag with gifts and envelopes of money.

Word spread fast in the village of Father's return and soon he was surrounded by long-lost relatives. His most important contacts were Grandpa's two cousins, one of whom was the village chief. Father wanted to see Grandpa's tomb, which took them a while to locate. After much scouring amid knee-deep grass, the village chief identified what appeared to be an unmarked grave and declared it to be Grandpa's. He had his children draw a detailed map and reaffirmed his promise to have it properly tended and to personally oversee arrangements for the burial of Grandma.

We were skeptical. All written records had been lost to wars and floods. How could he be sure that the unmarked grave was really Grandpa's? Father was impatient. "Let's have a little faith," he said. "Faith" is not a word Father used very often, and I think that, deep down, he shared our doubts, but he chose to believe.

Father had incurred an obligation by asking the village chief to watch over Grandpa's grave, though the enormity of that obligation was not readily apparent until a letter from the chief arrived the following spring, announcing that his son-in-law had been offered a job in our city and that his daughter would soon join her husband here. She was having some problems getting settled and the chief asked Father to help find his daughter a place to stay and a job to tide her over. Before Father could respond, the daughter was at our door. She was a peasant girl, who giggled a lot and spoke with a heavy Henan accent; some of her words had the same twang as Grandma's. My elder sister volunteered to make room for the new auntie by staying at the house of one of her friends. Father found her a temporary job, loading and unloading cooking utensils at his warehouse.

Fortunately, her husband found a dorm for the both of them and she was gone in a month. This auntie was just the first of many new aunties and uncles. How far did our family extend? Some came as tourists and used our house as a free hotel, some to request financial help, others to look for a job in the city. They thought Father was some big shot. My siblings and I grew weary of the constant disruption in our lives and made no attempt at courtesy. Father scolded me for being snobbish and ungrateful. "These are nice, honest people," he lectured. "Don't look down on them. They have put in a lot of effort to help keep Grandpa's grave."

Initially, Mother tried, greeting our relatives warmly and always cooking a big noodle meal, but the strain began to show and when three men claiming to be our relatives showed up at the door late one summer night, she'd had enough. Claiming to have a headache, she went out to join her friends, leaving my sister to make supper for our guests. Father took out some bedding and let them sleep in his office at work, hoping that, as farmers, they would be up early and be gone before his colleagues arrived. Sure enough, they were outside the house at six o'clock the next morning, waiting for their breakfast. A neighbor, aware of our situation, joked: "Your hotel business has been quite good lately."

Grandma used to complain whenever Mother's relatives came

to stay, muttering that Mother had given away too much money and gifts. "Most of the Huang family members died off and we hardly have anyone," Grandma said. Now that contact had been made with Grandpa's relatives, the tide had turned, and Mother took a jab at Father: "Didn't you say all of your Huang family members died during the famine?" Words were exchanged, voices were raised, and Father retreated to the courtyard.

But Mother wasn't finished and brought up her threats again. "Who would have known that we have to go through so much trouble to get your mother to Henan," she said, and turned to Grandma, who was sitting in her wicker chair under the pear tree. "I feel very tempted to just find a burial place outside Xi'an. You've been here for years, and this is where your grandchildren live."

Grandma barked: "I don't want to talk about death now. Even if I die, I don't want to be buried in this place; it's not my home!" Then, giving Mother a withering look, she came up with a new line against Mother: "I know how you are. If you could have your way, you wouldn't hesitate to wrap me up in a piece of cheap straw sheet and dump me in a furnace or on the side of the road."

Mother suppressed her anger and said to Father, "I feel very much at home here. It's a new society now. We can't follow every old rule."

Father disagreed. "All fallen leaves return to the tree roots," he said. "No matter how far you travel away from home, you have to go back."

"Fine," Mother said. "Go ahead and take your mother home. I'm not going to help!" And then she left to seek consolation among her friends in the neighborhood.

Despite Mother's claims, we children knew that she and Father never treated Xi'an as home. They made no effort to lose their accent or change what they ate. Their friends came from the same region of Henan, and whenever Mother met a woman who spoke with the accent of her hometown, she was welcomed in our house. Father even insisted that my siblings and I should marry people of Henan descent when we grew up. Occasionally, I even heard Father tell his friends that he and Mother would want to move back to our ancestral home after retirement, even though they had nothing there and hardly knew anyone except some distant relatives. That conversation flashes in my mind each time I hear some of my Chinese-American friends say that they never feel at home even though they have been in the United States for years. Some are saving money and plan to move back to their "homeland" after retirement.

After Mother left, Grandma blubbered to Father, "If you don't want to send me home after I die, maybe you should take me to our village while I'm still alive. I'll rent a room in our native village and will probably live longer without this evil woman around me." Then, she broke down. "I'm so afraid of death."

PART TWO

13.

THAW

Chairman Mao was dead, and his successor, Hua Guofeng, began to clean house in October 1976, starting with the "counterrevolutionary clique" led by Mao's wife, Jiang Qing, and three other radical Communist leaders. Known as the "Gang of Four," they were charged with conspiring against the Party and put under arrest.

Mother acted as if she had known all along that Mao's wife was a bad person. "She wore that black scarf and looked so distracted at Chairman Mao's funeral," she said. "I knew there was something going on." Father told her, "Don't get too smart with your observation; she is the enemy now, but what's going to happen tomorrow? She might come back as empress. The only thing certain about Chinese politics is that nothing is certain. You can be an honored guest today and locked up as a criminal tomorrow."

Father knew from experience to be cautious, but soon enough the catastrophes of the Cultural Revolution were blamed on Mao's wife and her clique, and it was as if Chairman Mao had slept through those dreadful years, unaware of and therefore blameless for the radical policies that had ruined China's economy and caused the deaths of millions of innocent people. The Party tried to right wrongs; with the fall of the Gang of Four, many former enemies became our comrades again, and those former counterrevolutionaries and capitalists turned out to have been good Communists all along. In my former elementary school, there was a counterrevolutionary, whose job was to do carpentry and repairs. We used to mock him all the time until, overnight, he became the school principal. We were told he had been a victim of the Gang of Four. The greatest surprise came when the verdict against Liu Shaoqi, the former president of China, was overturned. I grew up shouting "Down with Liu Shaoqi" or "Liu Shaoqi is a traitor and the biggest advocate of capitalism in China." Liu was beaten and imprisoned during the Cultural Revolution. He died a prisoner in Henan Province in 1969. In an incredible backflip, the Party told us in 1980 that Liu was really a remarkable Marxist and a great proletariat revolutionary. A great funeral was arranged, attended by all the senior leaders. Chinese politics is confusing most of the time, more so for a teenager, but even I could tell that China was changing for the better.

Even more shocking to me was the time when I came home one day and noticed that a gigantic statue of Chairman Mao had disappeared from a three-meter-high pedestal near the eastern entrance of Father's factory. Workers had taken the statue down and sent it away to be smashed. The Party had decided to end Chairman Mao's cult of personality and urged people to liberate their thinking. Not long after, I saw dozens of trucks parked outside Father's warehouse. The trucks were loaded with different sizes and shapes of buttons with images of Chairman Mao, which we faithfully wore on our chests every day, collecting and trading them like today's Pokémon cards. Barely three years after Chairman Mao's death, the government in Xi'an urged residents to dump the metal badges at a downtown recycling center and then shipped them over to Father's factory so workers could melt and recycle them to make cooking utensils and sewage pipes. According to a recent news report, China produced eight billion Chairman Mao badges in fifty thousand designs between 1966 and 1971. Before they were tossed into the furnace, Father carefully picked several unique designs from the pile and brought them home as collectibles, putting them in the drawer where he used to store all of his books banned by Mao.

For me, the most obvious sign of change was the relaxation of the food rationing system. The black market, where Father went secretly to buy sweet potatoes and wheat, became the "free market"—peasants everywhere peddled fresh vegetables, wheat, and pork. The communes were being disbanded and farmers could lease land and grow crops of their choice. So long as they fulfilled government quotas, they could sell the surplus at the market. It was good news for us; Father no longer had to worry about getting caught buying food so we might eat. White steamed buns, a symbol of China's happy socialist life, became a regular feature on our table.

Life also became more colorful. Old-time revolutionary propaganda movies depicting brave Communists fighting the cowardly Nationalists or defeating the evil Japanese invaders disappeared. Films from the 1950s with love themes and Hong Kong kung fu flicks attracted large crowds at the formerly deserted movie theaters. In 1978, the sweet voice of Deng Lijun, a Taiwanese singer, conquered the whole country; and I can liken her impact on China to that of Elvis Presley's on America. My classmates and I, who had been fed strident revolutionary songs such as "Socialism Is Good" and "I Love My Motherland" since childhood, fell under Deng's sappy spell—"The Moon Represents My Heart" and "Don't Pick the Roadside Wildflowers." A classmate's brother smuggled in a reel-to-reel tape from Hong Kong. Through my English-language teacher, I borrowed a large boxlike Grundig tape recorder from the school language lab with the excuse that we were practicing our spoken English and we gathered in our dorm. Despite the initial shushing, the volume was turned up, louder and louder, until it reached the ears of the deputy principal, who did not approve of using school equipment to listen to "unhealthy music." My English teacher bore the brunt of the blame. Beyond our school walls, people were jailed for dancing to Deng Lijun's songs, which only increased her allure, and the government finally gave up.

The 1970s may have been about to end in the West, but the

decade of fashion faux pas had barely begun in China and bell-bottom pants and long hair had invaded. For us, it came in the form of the musician daughter of our English teacher, who, as we exercised in the playground during our physical education class, walked past on a visit to her mother. All heads turned to her navy blue bell-bottom pants, which accentuated her figure in a way few Chinese boys could imagine. Soon several seniors at our school began wearing bell-bottoms and we all gave up haircuts. Our principal urged students to boycott the bourgeois lifestyle, threatening to take a pair of scissors to our long hair and wide pant legs if we did not correct our behavior. By the time I managed to beg Mother to make me more fashionable trousers, bell-bottoms were so common that I'd lost interest.

My younger brother didn't care for bell-bottoms, but he changed his hairstyle every other week. Father—who used to take us to a barber for a buzz cut twice a month when we were kids and claimed that long hair caused headaches—called my brother a hooligan. When my brother proposed opening his own hair salon after graduating high school to supplement the family income and help save for Grandma's funeral, Father flew into a rage. "We spent all this money and effort to protect our good feng shui so you could be blessed with a big future," he said. "What a waste; can't you think of an honorable and decent profession instead of running a business?" Merchants are ranked among the lowest of the low in Confucian thinking.

Father didn't like the cultural trends of the new era, but he was grateful that traditional Chinese opera had returned after a decade of being silenced. He dug out from his drawer a small homemade radio with a big battery box hanging loose from its back. The radio had been made for him by a friend in the mid-1960s and he would put the radio to his ear after work and listen through the static to the traditional operas. He seemed deaf to the static from his radio, but it increasingly annoyed Mother, and to avoid conflict he reluctantly took money from Grandma's funeral fund and bought a coveted Red Lantern radio, which cost him the equivalent of two months' salary. It was a big wooden box, with a colorful silklike fabric on the front. I liked that it could pick up shortwave frequencies. I soon found Voice of America's English news program, secretly popular among many students at my school. It was through it that I first heard about the murder of John Lennon and the silent vigils around the world in his memory. I could not fathom why Westerners mourned the death of a pop star as if he were a head of state like Chairman Mao. Listening to foreign broadcasts was still politically questionable. Father would only allow me to listen to Voice of America under his supervision. He had a carpenter build a lockbox on the only electric outlet in our house.

Soon radio was replaced by TV, which was becoming more accessible in 1978, and even families poorer than we were had a set, but Father refused to buy one, even though he would sometimes slip next door to watch Beijing or Henan operas at our neighbor's house. "Let's wait until better models come out and prices come down," he would say. "We can't squander money on luxury products. We need to prepare for Grandma's funeral." Mr. Yu, Father's company's sales director, had the biggest TV in the residential complex and large crowds would gather in his living room and sit in the windows to watch popular shows. When the American TV show *Man from Atlantis* reached China's airwaves, my younger brother was one of its many die-hard fans. On the night of the show, he would excuse himself from his homework saying he had to use the public latrine and return thirty minutes later, his jacket covered in dust from Mr. Yu's window. In the end, Father relented and bought an odd-looking discount set. When he wasn't home, he kept the electrical outlet locked.

As the big character slogans on the walls—REFORMING OLD TRADITIONS AND CUSTOMS—faded away, some traditional practices crept back into our lives, sometimes spectacularly and from quite unexpected quarters. In our residential complex lived Mr. Zhou, a floor sweeper at Father's company who scavenged dumpsters and landfills for paper and scrap metal. He had four children, all of them girls. When we heard firecrackers coming from his house, a huge crowd gathered. Zhou's eldest daughter was getting married to a neighbor's boy and the whisper was that he had gotten her pregnant, hence the hastily arranged wedding. Mr. Zhou silenced the gossips when the bride emerged from inside a red sedan chair carried by two relatives. I had only seen such things in movies about evil landlords who abducted beautiful girls from poor peasant families. The crowd gasped; old women covered their mouths in surprise. The bride wore a traditional red coat with plaited buttons down the middle. Her sisters walked behind the sedan, carrying red silk quilts embroidered with a phoenix and dragon. When the bride's parents stepped into view, the crowd roared. Zhou, with his hair brushed neatly on one side and dressed in neatly pressed gray polyester pants and a tailored blue Mao jacket, was the personification of pride. "Never underestimate the power of a garbage collector," Mother said. "He must have a fortune stashed away."

What would the Party secretary say about this revival of traditional wedding practices? "Things have changed," Father said. "The Party has realized that not all traditions are bad." He was right. Nothing happened to Zhou, who continued to sweep floors and rummage through rubbish.

Like weddings, traditional funerals, once scorned as a wasteful practice of a misguided past, became commonplace in the rural areas. In major cities such as Xi'an, burial was still banned, but enforcement was patchy in the suburbs. If one had the means to secure a piece of land, one had the means to bend the rules. In 1980, when a granduncle passed away, Father felt that as a Party member it would be inappropriate for him to attend because the funeral would be followed by a secret burial. Mother and I did go, and when the coffin was hoisted into the hearse, a group of women, Mother among them, cried and wailed—Mother was loud and very much in demand for relatives' funerals—as two dozen children dressed in white linen, including me, knelt in three lines. Firecrackers were lit, signaling the start of a procession that involved a dozen or so cars and trucks loaded with hundreds of wreaths and paper offerings of perfectly scaled gold bars to be burned so the deceased would not arrive in the other world empty-handed. To avoid the police, the procession stuck to side streets and fake money was scattered in its path for the ghost guards so they would allow easy passage. I hadn't realized the other world was as corrupt as the one in which I lived.

As access to transport became easier, Father began modifying his plan accordingly. He even managed to obtain permission to use one of the company clinic's two ambulances to transport Grandma's body. Dr. Yang, whom Mother had befriended years earlier, even suggested moving Grandma as she neared the end so she might die in her own village. He volunteered to come along and make sure she was kept comfortable during the journey, which road improvements had dramatically reduced in duration.

My older sister was also given a more prominent role, not something I would have expected when the plan was first launched. She had been dating a former classmate for two years. His parents came from a rural village on the outskirts of Xi'an. Mother and Father were opposed; they wanted her to marry into a city family, preferably someone with roots in Henan. It would also be a step down for her, from working at a state-run company to joining him at a small cooperative with far fewer benefits. My sister was a cunning person, a trait of hers I particularly liked because she had more than once been able to get us out of trouble when we were younger. With the help of her boyfriend's family, she presented Father with a proposal she knew he would find hard to resist: If she were to marry her boyfriend, Grandma would, through family connections, have access to the village cemetery for as long as was needed, so if something went wrong with the Henan plans, Father had a secure fallback position in place. Her relationship was allowed to develop.

In 1981 came news that threatened to derail Father's meticulous plans. The local government had earmarked the Huang family cemetery for reclamation and conversion into farmland.

Villagers were told to either level the tombs or remove them and their remains to a more remote location before the whole area was bulldozed. Father was against the relocation and said so in a strongly worded letter to Grandpa's cousin, the village chief, whose reply came via "giggling auntie," our nickname for the daughter we had helped years earlier. She said her father had fought local officials to preserve Grandpa's gravesite and had even lain down in front of the tractor sent to level the ground. The village chief saved Grandpa's grave, but had to bribe some local officials, she said. Father was touched by the village chief's "heroic act" and he wired money to cover the cost of the bribes.

The village chief suffered a heart attack in 1985 and Father took the news badly. He was the cornerstone of the plan. Father contacted Grandpa's other cousin, who assured Father he would carry on the task. I had met him when he came for a visit and he struck me as honest and less glib than the village chief. In return, Father brought his cousin's seventeen-year-old son to the city to live with us and found him a job.

Meanwhile, as Grandma approached eighty, her fear of death worsened. When relatives and friends dropped by for visits, Grandma would interrupt the conversation. "I'm so scared," she would say, followed by a nervous giggle. "I don't want to leave my grandchildren." Then, if Mother was not around, she would, in her whispering voice, accuse Mother of conspiring to get rid of her because she had become a burden to the family. Her frequent interruptions put our guests in an awkward position. Initially, some would try to listen and comfort her, but soon they all stopped visiting us.

Every now and then, if dizzy spells hit her, Grandma would remind us that "I will die any minute now." We indulged her. Late one night, she woke us up, howling that she was approaching her end. It was two days before the Lunar New Year. Upon her death, she advised Father to wrap her body with a piece of red cloth and temporarily store it inside the coffin. "I don't want my death to ruin your New Year celebration," she said. "Besides, your mother has prepared all that New Year's food and we can't let it go to waste. You can notify our relatives and handle my funeral afterward."

Then she had Father bring me over so she could leave me her last words. I knelt next to her bed, holding her hands tightly. I could see tears flowing across her temples. I sobbed and began to hope that Grandma would reveal some life-changing secrets like those dying revolutionaries in the movies: "You were an orphan. Your biological mother was a revolutionary martyr who was killed by the Nationalists. Grandma is your sole surviving relative!" That would probably explain why Mother spanked me so much. Or perhaps Grandma might leave me some money: "I have hidden some gold bars between the kitchen walls. Dig them out after I die and enjoy yourself. And don't share it with your annoying sisters." It seemed highly possible. For years, I had heard stories from relatives that Grandma had brought gold bars from Henan to Xi'an.

Grandma finally spoke up and I held my breath in anticipation. "You should keep practicing cooking. In this way, you won't have to suffer at the hands of your wife, like your father does." My sobbing stopped. I looked to see if Mother was around.

Fortunately, she had left to fetch Dr. Gao. Shaking his head with his usual look of disapproval, Father handed Grandma a glass of water. She brushed it away. "A dying person can't drink water. I might choke and leave this world without giving my last words to everyone."

Dr. Gao came in, looking sleepy and impatient. He felt Grandma's pulse. "Huang Mama, you are not dying. Your pulse is strong and you'll live to be one hundred." Grandma smiled. Before Dr. Gao left, he sent Father to pick up some sleeping pills for Grandma at the company clinic. By the time Father returned, Grandma was already snoring.

14.

MATRICULATION

At the height of Father's preoccupation with Grandma's burial, he hardly had any time for his children. His political-study meetings kept him late at work and once he was home, he would either be exhausted or entangled in the burial discussions or arguments with Mother. The only time we had his full attention was when we got into trouble in school and the teacher showed up at our door. After the teacher left, we would be punished. Several years in a row, Father skipped my annual parents' meeting with the excuse: "I know you'll do better and I needn't worry about you."

While I excelled at school without much parental supervision, my younger brother and sister did poorly and frequently received failing grades. Father assigned me and my elder sister to help with their studies but we were too busy with our own extracurricular activities. As a result, they were left on their own. In his teenage years, my younger brother joined a neighborhood gang. Often, when Father came home from work, he would encounter angry parents whose children had been beaten up by my brother. During his high school entrance examination, my brother managed to pass, but he missed the admission cutoff for the best school in the area by only two points. He ended up going to a neighborhood school with a high dropout rate. Without his receiving the proper coaching, his academic record deteriorated further.

In later years, as Grandma's situation remained relatively stable, Father started to compensate for his previous inattention, but it was too late. None of my younger siblings achieved the high test scores that would qualify them for college.

Conversely, I was more fortunate. Following my admission to the Xi'an Foreign Languages School, my parents' attitude toward me changed dramatically. Since I was only home on weekends, they treated me as if I were an honored guest. The spanking stopped. Mother always cooked special meals for me. Out of jealousy, my siblings began calling me the family's "endangered species" that needed special care and protection.

Father felt greatly relieved that his eldest son did not have to suffer in the remote countryside after graduation. School authorities had made it clear to my parents that students would have the opportunity to work as interpreters for senior leaders in Beijing. The promise stoked Father's hope that I might become somebody who would glorify the family.

As he prepared me for big things in life, Father urged me to follow all sorts of rules. I should speak slowly and confidently, and always walk with my back straight and eyes forward. "You look like a little old man searching for pennies on the ground," he said. "That's not the way a person who does big things walks." I still walk a little hunched over and with my head down, and I pick up quite a few pennies. It might amuse Father that they are considered lucky in America.

Starting in 1977, we no longer had to study half a day and then spend the rest of the time doing physical labor at a school-run factory or in the rural areas. Math, chemistry, and physics became popular subjects. Test scores were again about knowledge, rather than the ability to quote Chairman Mao. Our teachers no longer mentioned "settling in the rural areas and being a revolutionary successor." Our ultimate goal was to pass the test and attend universities. In our English class, we no longer had to learn the awkward English translations of Chairman Mao's teachings, such as "American imperialists are paper tigers." Instead, we could read about Snow White from a pirated version of a British textbook.

I thrived on the changes. At my new school, I excelled in both my science and social-science classes. At the end of each semester, when I handed Father my report card, he felt vindicated that he had always encouraged me to study hard while other parents gave up on their children's education in the Mao era.

In 1978, an article about the mathematician Chen Jingrun caught the imagination of Chinese high school students. Chen, one of the greatest mathematicians of the twentieth century, made a significant contribution to the Goldbach Conjecture, but nobody at school could explain what that was. All we knew was that it was a world-renowned number theory and Chen had gained glory for China. Suddenly everyone wanted to be a mathematician. I was obsessed with math. Agonizing over a particularly complicated math problem before going to bed one night, I managed to solve it in my dreams and decided I must be a genius. I thought of becoming a world-famous mathematician. Father read up on Chen and learned that the math genius had no life outside his work, no social skills, and would often forget to eat and sleep. The government eventually had to intervene and found him a wife to take care of him. Father noticed that I became absent-minded, losing my allowance money and misplacing my keys. He decided he did not want me to become a mathematician and when my teacher recommended that I transfer to a school for talented math students, he refused.

When I was in high school, Father seldom had time to intervene in what books I read, claiming that it was beyond his ability to help me. One day, I began reading the Chinese classic *Dream of the Red Chamber,* and I knew he had read it many times. To impress him, I tried to discuss the book with him. A look of horror crossed his face. "That is not a suitable book for you," he said. The main character was a dissolute dandy, Father explained. On the boy's first birthday, his father displayed an array of tools—including a pen, which was the mark of the scholar, and a sword, the tool of the warrior—to predict his future. Ignoring everything presented, the character grabbed some face powder and put it in his mouth. His father knew from then on that his son would be a useless good-for-nothing. He wastes his life flirting with girls and lets his family fall apart. "The book could have a bad influence on you," Father said to me. He warned me that the two things certain to prevent a person from being successful were women and money. "If you are too indulgent and greedy, you will get into big political trouble," he said.

Unlike parents and teachers in the West, who encourage children to stand out from the crowd, be confident, unique, and let their individuality shine, my parents insisted that I be *ting hua* or obedient and conforming, because "the gun will shoot the head of the flock." Speaking from his own experience, Father warned me, "Don't show off and be overly aggressive at school. Go with the flow. Otherwise, if anything goes wrong, you are likely to be a bigger target."

Time and again Father advised me to be humble, no matter what I might do in the future, and "walk with tail between legs." He recounted the story of Zhang Liang, an ancient strategist, who met a gray-haired old man at a river bridge—in most of Father's stories, the model is always a gray-haired old man—and the old man tossed his shoes onto the ground and ordered Zhang Liang to pick them up for him. Zhang did as he was told. The old man threw the shoes farther away. Zhang wanted to curse him, but his upbringing forbade him, so he fetched the old man's shoes a second time. The old man noted Zhang's humility and patience, and told him to be at the same spot the next morning. Zhang was late. The old man was upset and sent him home. Again the old man arranged a meeting, and this time Zhang gained his trust and he gave Zhang a book of military strategies that made him one of the great military strategists in China's history. The point of the story, Father explained, was to respect others because you never know what special talents they might have.

In the West, I see how parents lavish praise and encouragement on their children and put pictures of them on their desks. When their children fail, they comfort them and urge them on. This couldn't be further from my own experience. My parents, like many in China at the time, believed that praise led to arrogance and that criticism encourages children to aim higher. Throughout my school years, my academic performance was among the best in the class. Never once did I hear my parents praise me. Each year, when I brought home my report card showing I had come in first, they would say, "Your class is tiny. There's nothing special about it. In the real world, there are thousands of smart kids. You have no reason to be arrogant." When I joined the school basketball team, Father said, "You'd better practice hard because you are too short." In my teenage years, my mother would compare me to a neighbor's boy. "He's tall and good-looking. His mother doesn't have to worry about his marriage. You are short and ugly. You'd better be talented; otherwise you won't be able to find a wife."

The criticism sunk in; even now I can't stand to look at myself in the mirror. As a teenager, my foreign language skills made me a bit of a novelty and many of Father's colleagues wanted to meet me. I dreaded those meetings, afraid I would not be as good as they expected and would disappoint them. I came close to a nervous breakdown whenever I had any type of tests in school; I was sure I wasn't smart enough to pass.

My generation grew up in big families with limited resources. Many of us did not even know there was such a thing as birthday parties for children. If my parents happened to remember my birthday, I might get a boiled egg. We never had the luxury of private piano or violin lessons. In high school, I was a singer and a top runner. My parents never bothered to take time off to see me perform onstage or compete in races. Under the one-child policy, which came into force in 1979, children are treated differently now. Parents are overcompensating for what they lacked in their own childhoods. While her daughter was in senior high school, my younger sister, who felt neglected by my parents in her teenage years, gave up many of her social activities and stayed home every night to coach her daughter's studies. A friend of mine specifically cut short his business trip recently so he could attend his son's cello recital. I heard him call his son a genius after a rather good performance. In my days, the young man would have been told, "It's nothing and go practice more."

Most of my Chinese friends swear that they will never treat their children the same way we were treated as children. Nonetheless, we never see our parental put-downs as a problem. A Chinese lawyer friend told me that our lessons in humility made us tougher psychologically, a reminder that there is nothing special about us and we need to always work harder. He is a vocal critic of the overly attentive way that parents treat their children in China nowadays. "China is turning into a nation of brats and weaklings," he said. If Father were alive, he would probably utter similar sentiments.

In the many ancient stories that Father shared with me, an important measurement of success was the imperial academic examination, the passing of which opened the way for senior posts at the imperial court. In modern times, the imperial examination came in the form of the National University Entrance Examination, an effective and highly competitive merit-based system, through which students of all economic strata could enter college. I eagerly awaited my turn, which came in 1982.

In ancient times, scholars needed to memorize the Confucian classics to pass the rigorous tests required to serve at the imperial court. Thanks to Chairman Mao's anti-Confucius campaign, my classmates and I no longer studied the full Confucian classics, but our test was based on dozens of government-published textbooks on Chinese literature, history, geography, Marxist theory, and math. The emphasis was on rote learning, which discouraged students from being too creative and critical. "Our Party needs more obedient hard workers, not some troublemakers," Father used to say.

Since only a small percentage of high school graduates could enter college, our teacher lectured us with the well-known "devoting one Red heart and preparing for two outcomes" mantra, meaning that even if we failed the exam, we could still help with the social modernization program; everyone knew it was a lie. Those who failed would find it hard to land a job in a state-owned enterprise.

Initially, I didn't feel any pressure because I always found it easy to commit a textbook to memory and felt confident enough to play truant. In January, six months before the exam, I

THE LITTLE RED GUARD   •   163

volunteered every other night to help a friend's mother who had been hospitalized. My head teacher found out about this after my score had dropped to third place in the class during a mock test. Worried that I wouldn't be able to gain honor for our school, he contacted Father, blaming him for not giving me enough attention. Father began to monitor me closely. On weekends, Father insisted that I go to study at his office, which was free of the distractions of TV and Mother's loud conversations. He would lock the door from the outside and then came to "release" me after midnight. In the end, I could recite word for word the definition of the Marxist concept of "surplus labor" and the theories of how Communism was the gravedigger for capitalism, even though I barely understood what they meant. I can still recite the timeline of the American Revolution, from the Boston Tea Party and the battles of Lexington and Concord to the Declaration of Independence and the adoption of the Constitution. I didn't know how such knowledge would make me a more capable Communist, and the only time I use it is when I am watching *Jeopardy!*

In the first sultry week of July 1982, I took the examination—all the questions required textbook answers, and I had all the textbooks in my head. When the scores were published, I was among the highest in the province. I applied to study English literature at Fudan University in Shanghai, one of the most prestigious schools in China, but many relatives advised my parents to let me stay in Xi'an, because, as the oldest son, I had responsibilities to my parents and siblings. Father overruled their concerns. "A man should be able to go far for the big things in life and then come back to repay the kindness of his parents with his success."

Father considered my good luck to be the blessing of Grandpa and my ancestors, something he took very seriously. When the admission letter came, Father wanted to add another layer of paint to the coffin; Mother said, "Don't be so superstitious."

In my teenage years, I had always wanted to escape from my family, to get as far from Xi'an as I could, but when the time came to leave for Shanghai in September, I found it hard to say good-bye. Mother was the only one who had been to Shanghai, and she remembered the busy shopping streets and the bright neon lights. "Many young people in Shanghai long for bourgeois lifestyles—they pay a lot of attention to how they look. Don't be corrupted. Live simply and focus on your studies," she said.

Through a friend who was helping with Grandma's funeral plans, Father booked me a hard seat train ticket, which allowed me to stay in the less crowded sleeper section. "See, you also benefit from all those New Year's visits, not just your grandma." Father winked at me. When the train clanked and rumbled away from the station where my parents stood waving on the platform, I cried like a child. I had never felt so vulnerable. My letters home were all about how much I missed Xi'an and Grandma until Father wrote, telling me to focus on my studies. "Your letters make Grandma and Mother cry. Don't be too sentimental and make them sad. A real man places his career above his family. Get yourself a bowl of noodles. It will make you tough." I listened and stopped writing letters and, as fall turned into winter, Grandma receded in my mind, and the big city of Shanghai began to take up more and more of my time—even the strong chlorine taste of its water, which I had found revolting, began to taste normal to me.

In my first year in college, I tried to live up to Father's expectations, aiming for straight A's in all my required classes, and I became active in the Communist Youth League. Before long, the Party secretary of my department held a long talk with me, encouraging me to apply for Party membership, which he said was courting young people who were both Red (politically active) and knowledgeable (academically sound). Father was pleased with the news but warned me not to spend too much time on politics, which he said could be risky and fickle. He advised in a letter: "Intellectuals have always been scapegoats in past political campaigns. Be careful." My interest in the Party did not last long. When the second semester started, I became preoccupied with a different set of new ideas, which I found liberating.

In the early 1980s, the government's open-door policy had turned Fudan University into a hotbed of discussions about long-banned Western political and philosophical ideas, China's equivalent of glasnost. In criticizing the brutal excesses of the Cultural Revolution, many emboldened intellectuals urged the government to reexamine the applicability of Marxism in China and called for respect for human values and dignity under socialism. On campus, Communism was beginning to lose ground and students turned to Western philosophers such as Friedrich Nietzsche and Jean-Paul Sartre for guidance. Following the death of Sartre in 1980, Chinese scholars translated many of his essays and plays into Chinese. By the time I arrived in Shanghai, Sartre was treated like a pop icon. If a student did not read about existentialism or possess a copy of *The Studies of Jean-Paul Sartre*, a collection of his works in Chinese, he would be considered unscholarly and a loser. When possible, we peppered our conversations with Nietzsche's quote "God is dead" or Russian writer Fyodor Dostoevsky's "If God doesn't exist, everything else is permitted" in the same way that Red Guards cited Chairman Mao's words during the Cultural Revolution. In classrooms that were fully packed, I attended lectures on Sartre and Nietzsche organized by the philosophy department, which was expected to focus on Marxism. To escape censorship, the lectures were conducted in the name of "taking a critical view of Western philosophies to deepen our understanding and appreciation of Marxism," even though the professors were avid followers of Sartre. Initially, I often skipped my regular classes and showed up at lectures on existentialism merely for the sake of being seen as a person of substance. However, as the semester ended, many of the existentialist views, such as Nietzsche's "will to power" and Sartre's "authentic existence" began to make sense and resonate with me, despite the fact that my understanding of them was still limited. All of a sudden, I found the teachings that I had received from Father and my teachers in high school—filial piety, obedience, loyalty to the Party and striving for good grades—seemed outdated and irrelevant to my future. I longed for freedom without the constraint of a regimented life. I felt ready to make my own choices in life, acting on my own, not according to what my family or the government demanded.

Intoxicated as I was by these existentialistic ideas, I began resenting the letters from Father, who continued to dispense what I deemed to be "archaic" advice—concentrate on your studies, refrain from speaking your mind in public, and postpone dating girls until graduation. In one of his letters, Father mentioned the coffin, which he was planning to move out of our house because of Grandma's increasing phobia about death. It so happened that I had just seen a new stage production of a well-known Chinese play called *The Peking Man*, which portrayed a declining aristocratic family in Beijing at the beginning of the twentieth century. Onstage throughout the play was a coffin that resembled Grandma's, which had been made for a patriarchal figure in the family. The patriarch, a scholar and former official, spent his waning days recalling the luxurious years of the past, even as his family was disintegrating into chaos and facing financial bankruptcy. His sole comfort lay in the coffin, to which he added a new layer of paint every year in the belief that the more times a coffin was painted, the better his life would be in the afterworld. The play provided me with a perfect excuse to discuss Father's obsession with Grandma's coffin and educate him about my newly acquired philosophical tenets. In a letter home, I told Father about *The Peking Man*, calling the coffin in the play a symbol of suffocating and death-inducing "feudalistic moral and cultural values." I likened Father's obsession to that of the patriarchal character, who remained oblivious to the changes in the world. Then I declared to him that I was no longer interested in Grandma's coffin as well as its associated meanings. I wanted to live my own life. Then I regaled Father with what I had learned from Nietzsche—the three stages of the spirit. I said I wanted to be a camel, absorbing all the knowledge, questions, and sufferings in life. I wanted to be empowered like a lion, conquering fear, self-doubt, and adversities, and then have a fresh start, like a newly born baby, free from restrictions and worries.

I waited anxiously for Father's reply. Four months passed and I still heard nothing from him. A week before the summer break, Father finally sent me a short note and money for my train fare. In the note, he wrote in a tone that I construed as being sarcastic: "I can see that your mind is becoming very sophisticated. Your remarks about the meanings of life are beyond my grasp. Chairman Mao used to say, 'The more books one reads, the more reactionary one becomes.' He might be right. I know you want to live a free life, but in China, asking for too much freedom can land you in jail. Please concentrate on your classes and do not waste time reading those useless books. It doesn't matter if you want to be a camel or a lion, you still need to abide by the rules of society. If you are not careful, the government could crush you like a bug. Come home. Grandma misses you."

I felt the urge to write back with a more vehement response, but realizing that I needed money for a trip that I was taking that summer, I gave up. When I was at home in the summer, Father and I never mentioned Sartre or the coffin. One day, when a group of friends gathered at our house, we bantered about politics, especially about the recent gossip relating to Mao's indulgent private life. A friend who was attending a college in Beijing made a casual remark. "Old Mao was such an immoral dictator and a peasant bandit. He and the Party have done their share of ruining China." Father overheard his comments. Fear spread across his face. After my friends left, he closed the window, as he always did when sensitive political topics came up. ("The walls have ears," he would say.) Then he asked me not to repeat my friend's comments about Mao to others in school.

"What's so risky about the statement?" I argued. "The Party Central Committee has pretty much negated everything that Chairman Mao did."

"You think you are college educated and know enough about life," he said. "You have no idea of the severe political consequences of your irresponsible remarks. The Party still calls Mao a great leader, and who gives you the right to call him a dictator? Chairman Mao might have made many mistakes, but he is still revered by many. In our country, if you want to succeed, you'd better learn how to keep your mouth shut." I despised what I saw as his "spineless" political view. "Times have changed. Only old stubborn people like you are still afraid and stay loyal to the Party." I stopped short of using the phrase "old stubborn fools." With that diatribe, I left. When I returned home that night, Mother pulled me aside and whispered that Father had sobbed after I had left. "You are like a baby bird who thinks the feathers on its wings are fully grown," Mother lectured. "It's sad that you look down on us like this." I was remorseless and never apologized to Father.

What happened in the fall of 1983 proved Father's wisdom. The Party tightened its control and launched an "anti–spiritual pollution campaign" to stem the spread of decadent Western liberal ideas, which they believed had undermined the supremacy of the Communist Party and led young people astray. Party leaders blamed the rising crime rates in China on the influence of bourgeois extreme individualism and Western imports such as pornography and Western hairstyles and clothing. As a result, books and lectures on Sartre and Nietzsche were banned. Many liberal-thinking writers and scholars were denounced. In Xi'an, I was told that many young people who organized private intimate dance parties and shared pornographic tapes with friends were sent to labor camps.

Father was relieved to hear that the campaign did not affect the overall student population at Fudan. I regretted my earlier outbursts at home, but I was too proud to tell Father that he was right. Fortunately the campaign was short-lived. Worrying that it could escalate into another Cultural Revolution, many moderates within the Party who had suffered tremendously in the Mao era petitioned senior leader Deng Xiaoping to limit its scope. In the summer of 1984, the Party's efforts to eliminate spiritual pollution gradually fizzled out. By then, my own interest in existentialism had also faded. However, the concepts of freedom and choice had been ingrained in my mind. I felt that I had found a way to live for myself.

15.

WESTERNIZATION

I crouched in my seat in the back of a Boeing 707, clutching a plastic bag as the plane sputtered in the fog over London. I closed my eyes, trying to calm my stomach and my mind, which was filled with a mixture of excitement and fear. Two years into my undergraduate studies, I was headed to the United Kingdom to study and learn from the former foreign colonialist who, after China's thirty-year isolation, were now our friends and models for modernization. We were to master the English language and apply our new skills to building a prosperous China. Back in the 1970s, my high school principal said foreign languages were weapons to fight our enemies; under Deng Xiaoping, our reformist leader, language became a tool to help us emulate them.

When I first heard Shakespeare in 1980, I thought "To be or not to be . . ." was from the *Analects of Confucius*. My early attempts to penetrate his work in Chinese were thwarted by the flowery, archaic language of the 1930s translation in the school library. Fortunately for me, a cinema in Xi'an was showing Laurence Olivier's *Hamlet*—the famous Chinese actor Sun Daolin dubbed Olivier's dialogue—and I found a connection; it was like one of Father's stories about the bloody power struggles of the Chinese imperial court. I didn't realize foreigners also believed in ghosts. Shakespeare was poetry. When old Polonius advises "Give thy thoughts no tongue, / Nor any unproportion'd thought his act . . . / Give every man thy ear, but few thy voice: / Take each man's censure, but reserve thy judgment" I heard echoes of Father. With new understanding, I retrieved *Hamlet* from the library and read it so often that I could recite "I loved Ophelia. / Forty thousand brothers / Could not / with all their quantity of love / Make up my sum" to girls in my class.

Father couldn't figure out how I could help modernize China by studying Shakespeare. "If an engineer studies abroad, he comes back and designs new machines that help peasants harvest more crops, but what can you do with Shakespeare?" I understood his reticence—in China, words, no matter how pretty, were the property of propaganda. However, in 1984, when few students were allowed to study abroad, having a *liu xue sheng*, or "student overseas," was a tremendous honor for the family. Father was happy. His company sent him to Shanghai to spend a week with me before my departure.

The authorities tried to buffer us from the culture shock we were about to undergo with intensive political and cultural study sessions so we wouldn't betray our motherland by defecting and embarrass China. It was hard to prepare anyone for their first encounter with a paper napkin or plastic knives and forks or unlimited supplies of Coca-Cola or the simple thrill of an airplane. I was twenty, doing things my parents could never dream of doing.

My first impression of Great Britain was that it was green; I had never seen so much lush grass, and I had trouble comprehending that its sole purpose was to be cut so it could grow again and please the eye. I grew up in the dust bowl of northwestern China and later lived in the polluted, densely packed city of Shanghai. In China, land not built on or being farmed was dirt. My knowledge of London was based almost entirely on the novels of the revolutionary realist writer Charles Dickens. I was expecting Oliver Twist, running around with a group of beggars on streets lined with smoke-spewing chimneys.

I remembered Father's first trip to Shanghai and how awed he was by its tall buildings and neon lights, how he'd jokingly called it a decadent capitalist city. In comparison to London, Shanghai was an ugly duckling.

My mind was able to adjust to the conflict between perception and reality, but I was entirely unprepared for my first visit to a supermarket, Morrisons in Leeds. As a child, we had been repeatedly told that China was rich and that we should pity the poor oppressed masses of the West. Yet here, as my eyes scanned aisles and aisles of merchandise in rainbows of packaging, was so much food I nearly went into shock. Packages of uncooked chicken already cut into pieces, beef, lamb and mutton, pork, vegetables of root and leaf and stalk, drinks in cans and bottles and cartons. In the cookie aisle, I lost the ability to move. There were so many shapes and sizes and colors. I remembered a childhood story about how some Western tourists were taken to a restaurant in Beijing and treated to Peking duck and white wheat buns. In return for the kindness of the Chinese people, the grateful guests brought out some dry dark bread and presented it as a gift. Our leaders gracefully accepted the gift and then dumped it in the garbage. In the new China, people no longer ate poor people's dark bread. We could afford big white buns, but we needed to save money and help the poor in the West. When I wrote to Father, I told him that people actually paid more for dark bread than white because it was better and healthier.

The early 1980s was a grim time for the UK. The British miners, under the leadership of Arthur Scargill, were on strike over mine closures. The yearlong miners' strike caused deep divisions among the students at my host university. Some students put up antigovernment posters and staged rallies in support of the miners. Others tore the posters down and rallied against the power of trade unions. On the kitchen wall of the flat I stayed in was a magazine portrait of Prime Minister Margaret Thatcher surrounded by pictures of topless girls from page three of *The Sun*, a tabloid owned by Rupert Murdoch. I was mesmerized by a new

TV show, *Spitting Image*, which used puppetry to satirize the British establishment, including the queen and the prime minister, and took shots at the hypocrisy of many world leaders. As a Chinese citizen, I had no experience with open displays of disrespect for leadership, but as the true sign of fluency in another language is to be able to laugh at the jokes of another culture, I relished this freedom. When my fellow students invited me to join rallies in support of the miners, I was nervous about participating in what were essentially demonstrations against the government and tried to stay on the sidelines, but when nothing happened to the students, I became more actively involved. Again, the freedom was exhilarating.

I had a hard time with my literature classes; since the development of critical thought was not encouraged in China, we learned to take notes and memorize whatever we were taught. In the UK, we met once a week with our tutor to discuss Shakespeare or the work of a contemporary writer. Then, we would go away and do some research and come back with an essay on the writer or a particular book. I struggled with the essays and left them until the last minute, writing through the night, drinking cups and cups of instant coffee and agonizing over my words. At the end of the semester, my overall score for English literature was only a B+. As if that were not humiliating enough, I failed miserably in my final English competency exam. Students were asked to write an essay about the impact of TV on young people. I did what I had been taught to do in China—I simply copied from memory an article that my teacher had used in our class. Impressed with my own amazing memory, I was expecting high scores. When the result came, I was stunned that I had scored an F, a first in my life. I was too ashamed to tell Father. Fortunately, he never inquired about my academic scores. Having heard stories about how some Chinese scholars or artists had defected to the West following their visits, Father was concerned that he might lose his eldest son to what the government called the "decadent world of capitalism," especially after I began describing enthusiastically the wonderful things that I had seen in the UK. In fact, the thought of defecting never occurred to me. I wrote to him how hard it was for a Chinese student to find a job and survive in the UK, which was deep in a recession. Father remained unconvinced. Citing a popular Chinese saying, Father urged me not to betray the motherland: "A son never rejects his own mother simply because she is ugly and poor," he wrote. "Besides, your Grandma misses you terribly."

With the onset of the winter, I began missing Grandma. At Christmas, our teacher assigned us the Bible as a work of great literature since many of the books covered in the curriculum contained biblical references. I found the biblical tales fascinating. I attended several Sunday services at an Anglican church and found the Christian idea of the heaven that exists after death to be soothing. If Grandma accepted Christian faith, knowing that she might ascend to such a heaven, she would not be as scared of death as she was then, I thought.

I stayed with a British couple in Oxford over the holiday. Both the husband and wife were teachers. They were my parents' age and had two children. There were lively discussions of politics at the dinner table, and the parents allowed their children to express their opinions, something we were not permitted to do at home. In the face of such lively challenges, I think Father would have been too scared to speak. The couple liked to take walks and I went with them. The couple held hands as they walked, occasionally kissing each other affectionately or snuggling in closer for warmth. I thought of my own parents, who had never showed even the smallest sign of intimacy. Marriage was just a work unit for taking care of the old and raising children.

Even though I had often voiced skepticism about the Communist ideology while I was in China and had avidly read many Chinese government–banned books and magazines written by dissidents overseas at my university library in the UK, I turned nationalistic in the presence of my British classmates and friends. Years of indoctrination by the Party could not easily be undone. At dinners or parties, in any group gathering, I heard myself fiercely defending China and Communism in the face of what I perceived to be the arrogant and prejudiced views of British colonialists. When the daughter of a wealthy British businessman in Hong Kong railed against the decision in 1984 by the British government to return Hong Kong to China in 1997, I forgot Father's advice and got into a loud argument with her. She had said the ordinary people of Hong Kong, Britain's last colony, were happy with the status quo. "How would you know what ordinary people in Hong Kong want?" I said. I might have had a glass of wine or two; I was rarely so bold. "You rich capitalists live in rich secluded areas above the masses. What gives you the right to speak on behalf of the ordinary people in Hong Kong?" Some of our fellow students applauded; others remained silent. After the military was sent into

Tiananmen Square in June 1989, my earlier nationalistic take on the Hong Kong handover changed; I became concerned about the erosion of civil liberties on the island.

My views sometimes put me in a difficult position during my stay in the UK. As head of the Communist Youth League, I was designated as leader for our small group, which mostly meant delivering thanks on behalf of our group for any generosity bestowed on us or courtesy extended to us. We all saw ourselves as representatives of China, not as individuals. When a member of our group wanted to return a camera he had bought after trying it out for two weeks, he was so worried that the manager might think badly of the Chinese people that he pretended to be Japanese, even though the sales slip stated he was within his rights under the store's return policy. When one of our students got drunk and made a fool of himself at a party, the others woke me and insisted that I go get him so he didn't "embarrass the Chinese people." I went and apologized on his behalf, but was met with puzzled looks and more than one person said gently, "Hey, he's just having fun." I wonder sometimes at the depth of my innocence and how others must have perceived me—as a Communist spy, maybe.

I was invited by some British friends to see the film *1984*, starring John Hurt and Richard Burton. What I saw was another example of western propaganda against Communism and disliked it intensely. When I read George Orwell's classic twenty years later, I was struck by its enduring significance and—with its having been published in 1949, the year the Communist Party took control of China—its prescient portrayal of totalitarian rule.

Upon my return to Shanghai in 1985, I wrote a report to the department, and essentially to the Party, praising our host country's remarkable culture and the abundance of material wealth and advanced technology. At the same time, I criticized the disparity between rich and poor; attributed the large number of punks—the influence of which still resonates—to the decadent bourgeois lifestyle; and used the conflicts in Northern Ireland to justify China's control of Tibet. I said nothing about the political, social, and cultural freedom, nor did I mention how I longed for the day Chinese television could broadcast programs poking fun at our leaders without someone being jailed or executed.

Father was thrilled that I didn't defect and relieved to perceive that my thinking had not been poisoned by my exposure to the West. He was prouder still that I had saved some of my stipend and bought him a Japanese-made color TV, which was not available to ordinary families in China. I gave Grandma a box of Twix chocolates, which she hid for months until they all melted. I bought Mother a sweater, but when she put it on, she noticed a small hole—I had bought it at a Christmas sale—and, embarrassed, I told her to throw it away. She wore it the next day, discreetly covering the hole as she showed it off to friends.

While I was in the UK, my older sister was married. With the austere Mao era behind us, my parents were adamant that the wedding follow the traditions and customs of Henan, similar to what we would do with Grandma's funeral. Since my sister protested, citing that she was a Communist Party member and grew up in Xi'an, mother and daughter consented to a compromise. My sister was married in what she described in her letter to me as a mixture of Mao-era simplicity and "strange" old traditions.

Since the wedding took place on a Sunday and all the neighbors would be present to watch the wedding procession, Mother advised my brother-in-law not to cut corners on gifts to our family and demanded that he borrow a car, a rare luxury in those days, to transport the bride and other relatives to the ceremony. She did not want to lose face in front of our neighbors.

Tradition dictated that the ceremony take place before noon (afternoon weddings are for second marriages). The groom showed up in his navy blue suit. He had managed to borrow an old beat-up jeep and a bus, and, based on Mother's instructions, ostensibly carried four types of gifts for the neighbors to see— two bottles of expensive liquor and two cartons of expensive cigarettes for our family, even though Father did not smoke or drink. He also bought a kilo of beef (taking a daughter away is like taking a piece of flesh from the mother) and a kilo of lotus roots (a play on the Chinese wedding phrase "separated but still connected"). My younger siblings blocked the entranceway and hid my sister's shoes. The groom had to beg his way through with bribes of money in red envelopes. Inside the house, the groom knelt down in front of Grandma and my parents, thanking them for raising my sister. In return, Mother followed a Xi'an tradition by presenting him with four poached eggs in a bowl. The eggs had been mixed with hot peppers, sugar, vinegar, and bitter herbs, representing all the flavors in life—sweet, sour, bitter, and spicy. The groom cringed but swallowed them down, showing that he was willing to take on all the flavors in life with my sister. Then Mother quietly tucked into my sister's hand a red envelope containing all the money that was supposedly given to the family by the bridegroom, and asked her to keep it as rainy-day cash.

The groom "snatched" the bride, who was dressed in a red polyester suit, and drove off in the jeep. Friends and relatives were bused to the ceremony, officiated by the Party secretary from my brother-in-law's company. Bowing to the groom's parents and company officials, the couple vowed to be a "harmonious revolutionary couple." His family paid for the wedding banquet that followed.

By the end of the evening, the newlyweds breathed a sigh of relief that it had all gone smoothly, free of complaints from Grandma and Mother. On their beds, they found peanuts and dates to symbolize "giving birth to both boys and girls early." With the one-child policy, it was really wishful thinking, but my sister didn't disappoint. Soon after I returned home from the UK, she gave birth to a boy.

Things were changing fast. English was becoming a valuable skill in the new era, not least of all in Xi'an, which began opening to foreign tourists in the late 1970s. Initially, Westerners had to stay at a couple of government-designated hotels, such as the People's Hotel, a Soviet-style domed building constructed in the 1950s. They were confined to visiting particular designated sites: the terra-cotta warriors; a school filled with "happy" children dancing and singing revolutionary songs; and "friendship stores," where they could buy silk, rugs, and traditional ceramics, with hefty markups and priced in "foreign exchange certificates." We children were taught to report any foreigner we saw wandering the backstreets, taking pictures. We were told those Westerners wanted to tell lies about China. Even so, I would secretly hang around the People's Hotel and try to strike up conversations with tourists to practice my English. Each time I got someone talking, we would be surrounded by curious onlookers, most of whom had never heard this strange language. It wasn't long before someone reported to the school that a classmate of mine had accepted gifts and asked a Japanese man to buy his father foreign-brand cigarettes at the friendship store. We were banned from the People's Hotel because we had made the government lose face by begging foreigners to buy cigarettes.

By the early 1980s, people had grown more comfortable with the presence of foreign tourists. Associating with them was no longer considered dangerous, and they afforded many opportunities for an enterprising local. Father remained prudent, his customary position whenever rules were relaxed in China. "If the policy changes, your connections with foreigners would ruin the political careers of your siblings," he warned me.

In the summer of 1985, an English woman who taught at my university wanted to come to Xi'an with me to see how "ordinary people" lived. Father, after much prodding, talked to the company's Party secretary, who became worried that the relatively poor conditions of our residential complex might tarnish the glorious image of our new socialist China. He recommended I host my teacher at a fancy restaurant downtown, so I lied to him and said the real interest of the teacher was the company because she wanted to learn about socialist production. The Party secretary swallowed this and ordered all the workshops cleaned and walls painted, and hung a big poster at the entrance, saying WELCOME OUR FOREIGN FRIENDS TO OUR FACTORY AND OFFER GUIDANCE. My family was moved, temporarily, to a big apartment in a newly constructed building and one of our new "neighbors," a chef, dropped by to prepare a sumptuous meal. The Party secretary and a group of people I hardly knew showed my teacher around the company. Out of politeness, she feigned interest and asked many questions; her hosts were delighted.

Mother liked the new apartment and refused to move out until the company found us a bigger place to live. The company's housing committee rejected her request, but Mother wouldn't give in. Noticing that several neighbors had been assigned new apartments after wining and dining key housing committee members, Mother chose to follow suit, but Father was reluctant to participate, saying that he didn't drink and wouldn't know how to entertain those officials, most of whom were big drinkers. Mother recommended I sit at the table to assist Father. On Mother's insistence, he acquiesced and promised to invite his supervisor and the housing officials over a week after the Lunar New Year. Mother spent a bundle on liquor and meat. The table was set and Father came back with six guests—all of whom were his friends, and none had anything to do with housing. Mother's face turned ashen. "I tried inviting my boss and other company officials, but no one was available. I didn't want your efforts to be wasted," Father explained after Mother had pulled him into the kitchen. "Besides, all these friends have promised to help with the funeral plan." Mother almost screamed at him. "All you remember is your mother's funeral. I guess we'll be stuck living in a pigsty for the rest of our lives."

Seeing that she could not rely on Father's support, she set out on her own, pestering individual housing committee members every week until they avoided her like the plague. Her relentless maneuvering paid off and, in the spring of 1985, we were assigned a two-bedroom unit on the first level of a different building with indoor plumbing. Grandma's chamber pot, once borne with a degree of honor to the communal latrine each night, was ditched, but there was no place for her coffin. Father, who had remained neutral during Mother's housing campaign, redeemed himself by moving the coffin to a discreet corner of one of the company warehouses, shielded from view by stacks of bricks. Grandma applauded the idea, saying that she did not have to be reminded of her funeral every day.

In 1986, I graduated from the university and became an employee of the government, which reasoned that, having paid for our education, it was entitled to assign graduates jobs until it got back its investment. Before graduation, I was approached about working as an assistant in foreign affairs for an important Communist leader. If I did well, it would put me on the fast track for a career in politics. I telephoned Father and he responded without even a pause. "No," he said. "If that Communist leader falls from his position, your future will also be ruined." He had me turn down the assignment and that left me with only one option, which was to return to Xi'an to teach at a local university.

Father's stance cost him: The children of several colleagues landed more glamorous jobs in Beijing and he lost his bragging rights, but he liked that I was home.

Xi'an was a bastion of conservative ideas—many of Mao's veteran revolutionaries held power there—and it surprised me that, in 1986, it was among the first in the inland regions to embrace the economic and political change that was sweeping the nation. People became obsessed with *zuo sheng yi*, "doing business," or as Father translated it, "speculation and profiteering." In his eyes, it was the black market dressed up in gray. Mother regaled me with tales of neighbors who had made fortunes engaging in new capitalistic ventures: The second son of Mr. Hou had gone to the southern city of Guangzhou and brought back several hundred color TVs and refrigerators, which he sold to retail stores in Xi'an. His mother now wore twenty-four-karat gold and boasted about her son all the time. Father interrupted: "If everyone is selling stuff, who's manufacturing it?" Mother ignored him. Father's niece sold dumplings and noodles in the Red Lantern District— a vibrant night market that sprang up selling all sorts of Xi'an specialty foods—and made more money at night than she did working her hotel day job. "Your father is so stubborn and incompetent," Mother complained. "He won't do anything."

Like Mikhail Gorbachev's perestroika in Russia, China introduced market reforms in the mid-1980s by first easing price controls on food and vegetables. The measures led to many problems. "You go out in the morning and the tomatoes are twenty fen a kilo," Mother said. "You go back in the afternoon, the price is thirty fen. What kind of system is this?" She reminded Father that the Communists used to condemn the unbridled inflation of Nationalist rule in the 1940s. Who is creating inflation now? Father told her not to complain, but I could tell he shared her sentiment.

Everyone was doing business because Deng Xiaoping said, "Getting rich is glorious"—everyone, that is, except my brother. A former classmate of mine quit his job at Father's company, went to the coastal cities to purchase trendy clothes, and resold them at a clothing market downtown. He asked my brother—he had a flair for such things—to go into business with him, but Father intervened, threatening to disown him. "Don't try to embarrass the family. You don't know how lucky you are to have that job with an iron rice bowl. Those swindlers will be caught sooner or later." My brother became a top manager at Father's company in the late 1990s, but the iron rice bowl was broken and the company went bankrupt after state subsidies were withdrawn. He runs a small spin-off company salvaged from the rice-bowl wreckage, but he still blames Father for ruining his chance to be his own man.

Father was entering his phase of complacency; he could breathe a little easier now that his four children were making their own lives. My younger sister worked as an archivist after graduating from night college; my elder sister excelled in her job; I was a teacher and raking in money moonlighting as an English tutor; my brother, though often the target of Father's frowns, was at least working.

I accepted my fate and eased into my new job at a teacher's university. Most of my students had grown up in the rural areas in the northwest and had seldom ventured out of their province. They looked up to me—someone who had studied in Shanghai and the UK—as their window to the world. In my Introduction to the English Literature class, I talked to a roomful of more than seventy students about Shakespeare, Virginia Woolf, and even George Orwell. For my Western Culture class, I showed them the tapes of Hollywood movies such as *The Godfather* and played the recordings of Beethoven's symphonies. The department's Party secretary said I was straying from preprepared teaching material and switched me to introductory English language teaching, but my students staged a ministrike and got me back.

It was a profitable time for English teachers all over China, and Xi'an in particular. The unique attraction of its terra-cotta warriors made it a top destination for foreign tourists, who swarmed the streets. Locals soon realized that English was the key to joining this boom. High school graduates wanting a job in one of the many hotels popping up all over the city needed two things: to be at least five foot ten, an important measure of good looks; and have a basic understanding of English. They could do nothing about the former, but they were prepared to pay whatever it cost for the latter. Even the small vendors selling souvenirs wanted English training so they could say, "Cheap, cheap, ten yuan" for one mini-replica of terra-cotta soldiers. Thousands of college students were eyeing graduate schools in the United States and Europe, and competed for the limited number of exit visas the government allowed. Many government officials and company executives found that English was now a requirement for future promotion. As a result, language schools flourished. Even university

professors and lecturers who had long held themselves as among
the elite residents of the academic ivory tower could not resist
the lure of money and anyone with a language qualification was
soon "piggybacking" or moonlighting. As a Fudan graduate, I
did not come cheap, and I was in such demand that I constantly
missed my Wednesday political-study sessions. More than once I
walked into a classroom late and taught for an hour oblivious to
the fact that they were not my students.

Years of Communist education became like the ancient artifacts
inside the tombs of China's emperors in Xi'an—they crumbled
into dust if exposed too long to the open air. "Contributing your
wisdom and efforts to the country's modernization drive" for the
country was replaced by earning big bucks for oneself and the Party's influence faded. Like everyone in China, I dutifully followed
the country's new economic mantra—make money and get rich.

Each payday, I would hand over a wad of cash to Father to
lock in the old desk drawer for Grandma's burial fund. "Didn't
I tell you to study hard and go to college?" Father would lecture
my brother. "Without education, you will never make it big." My
brother shot back: "Aren't you a model worker yourself? Didn't
Chairman Mao say the working class is the vanguard of the Revolution?" Father was at a loss for words. I could tell he was struggling with his belief in the Party. I earned in two months more
than he made in a year. The inequality shocked him. Father was
not alone in feeling betrayed by the system. He put away the red
certificates he had earned over the years. He even took down the
old portraits of Chairman Mao and Premier Zhou Enlai.

More and more, the health of Grandma, now eighty-four,

occupied Father's mind. In the autumn of 1986, he put her on the back of his bicycle and pedaled to a hospital after seeing blood in her urine. She was diagnosed with ovarian cancer, but the doctor said that, given her advanced age, the tumor wasn't life threatening and the surgery and chemotherapy would only make what was left of her life extremely uncomfortable. His prescription: "Let nature take its course." We prepared for the worst. Three months went by and nothing happened physically, but we could tell she was losing her mental faculties and it was painful for me to watch this tough yet caring and considerate woman drift in and out of awareness. In those days, none of us had heard of Alzheimer's. Father described Grandma's condition in his own unique way. "Life is a cycle," he said. "Grandma cared for you when you were a baby. Now that she has become an 'old child,' it is time to care for her."

Grandma had her lucid moments and she seemed to use most of them to either pester Father with her fear of death or obsess about my unmarried status; when would I make her a great-grandmother? When a girl I had grown up with came to visit one afternoon, Grandma found an excuse and joined her on the couch, looking her up and down. After she left, Grandma took my hand and said: "She has a big round face and big eyes. She's good to marry. She looks like she can have many babies." I laughed and lied that she was already married. When the girl called again the next day, Grandma refused to let her in. "My grandson is not home," she said, and slammed the door. "Why did you do that?" I asked her. "If you are not going to marry her, why bother?" she said.

As her mental condition deteriorated, any semblance of courtesy she had shown Mother in the past vanished. She kept up a stream of complaints, real and imagined: that she was made to sleep on the hard floor, though she had slept peacefully through the night on the new mattress I had bought her, and that Mother had paid a carpenter to prepare a coffin years before because she couldn't wait for Grandma to die. In her mind, Mother was "heartless" and "mean" and she would rant without provocation to relative and friend and stranger alike. More disturbing was her belief that Mother was trying to steal me, her eldest grandson, last of the Huang line. She would wake at midnight and ask for me. If I was staying at the teacher's dorm, she would scream and howl, cursing Mother for hiding me away. Neighbors would wake. Mother would be humiliated. Grandma would go back to sleep as if nothing had happened. "It's easy for you to say," Mother would protest when I urged her to stay calm. "The whole neighborhood thinks I'm an evil daughter-in-law."

In a culture where people never aired their dirty laundry in public, Grandma took her case to every passerby. She would scoop coins from a jar I used for small change and beg neighbors to buy her something to eat because Mother was withholding food from her. Without knowing Grandma's mental condition, the daughter of a neighbor thought this venerable old woman was being mistreated and reported Mother to the neighborhood committee, which Mother used to chair.

My elder sister moved Grandma to her apartment to give Mother a break and she behaved herself for the first day or so, but the balcony frightened her and we were summoned to come fetch her. As Mother joined my sister in the kitchen to prepare some lunch, Grandma, who was hovering close by, whispered to me: "Make sure your mother doesn't steal anything from your sister." I sighed.

As she became bedridden, we children took over her bathroom needs and washed her clothes. When I hung out the laundry, neighbors would say, "What a filial grandson!" I never heard anyone praise Mother.

Saddened by Grandma's mental deterioration, Father started to fine-tune the funeral plan. Before the Lunar New Year in 1988, Father wanted me to visit those relatives and friends involved in Grandma's funeral. "With Grandma's situation, it's important that you and I go together to show that we appreciate their help," he explained. I had planned a trip with my students and told him, clearly, that I no longer wanted any part of those visits. Before he lost his temper, I had already bolted for the door. When I returned a week later, Father refused to talk to me. I secretly felt lucky to have finally escaped that chore. I did not know it was Father's last New Year.

16.

LOSS

On New Year's Eve in 1988, Mother knit red belts for me and Father to wear to keep us safe from disaster. It was the Year of the Dragon, the birth year for both of us. With the previous Dragon Year, 1976, marked by the death of Mao and a devastating earthquake, everyone was unusually nervous.

In February, Father had turned sixty. My older sister had planned to cook an elaborate dinner and invite close relatives over, but Mother was against the idea, saying it was unlucky to celebrate his longevity while Grandma's health was increasingly in question. Instead, I took Father to Shanghai after the New Year. He told me that he had enjoyed travel before he was married, though I don't think he ever went anywhere for pleasure after he began our family. "I had to focus my financial resources on raising you children and preparing for your Grandma's funeral," he said.

In the spring, Father suffered a terrible setback at work. For two years, he had worked on a program to recycle scrap metal from the workshops and saved the company tens of thousands of yuan. The bosses were fulsome in their praise for his initiative and announced Father would get a promotion and raise. Instead, the promotion went to a woman who was a close friend of the Party secretary and the company leadership split the savings among themselves. Father was less concerned about the "theft" than the humiliation.

"Too many cadres use their positions of influence to enrich themselves at the expense of those they are supposed to serve," said Father. It was hard to believe those harsh words came from him. He had also begun to act strangely, walking around the house, muttering to himself and outdoing Mother in comparing Communists and the defeated Nationalists: "The Communist Party won China because the Nationalists were too corrupt and had lost the support of ordinary folks. The more we reform, the more we seem to resemble the Nationalists."

I attempted to help him snap out of his funk. "The promotion was only worth 6.5 yuan per month. Why fuss over a small amount of money? I can give you some extra cash each month to make up for the loss," I said. Father took great offense at what he perceived as my arrogant remarks: "You just don't understand. It's a matter of principle." Feeling that my good intention was grossly misunderstood, I muttered the Chinese equivalent of "whatever" and ended the conversation.

I too was unhappy in my work. I craved a change and pondered my next step. In the summer, while I was working as a tour guide at the Sheraton Hotel in Xi'an, an American left me a paperback to read and I knew what I wanted to do. The book was *All the President's Men* by Bob Woodward and Carl Bernstein. We had been taught that Richard Nixon was the greatest president of the United States, and to learn that this was not so, that he was corrupt and that he was overthrown by a newspaper, was all deeply unsettling. Despite everything we had been taught, here was a political system in which a pair of reporters could bring down a president. I wanted to try journalism. Fudan University had a graduate-level international journalism program and I took the entrance examination. In April 1988, I received my acceptance letter. I thanked Mother for her red belt.

Father's situation, however, continued to decline. He had developed a nonstop cough sometime around May. He never smoked, which I think had something to do with a relative's addiction to opium. Father had watched him smoke his family into destitution. Mother suggested tuberculosis, which had killed Grandpa and might have lain dormant in Father's own lungs all this time. He attributed his cough to the thick lead dust that he inhaled at work. The company distributed masks and gloves, but like most of his colleagues, he seldom wore them and sold them to rural hospitals for extra cash. When the coughing kept him up all night long, Father would shake a bottle of herbal syrup, take a sip, and say there was nothing to worry about. After each new bout of coughing, his forehead would be beaded with sweat. He refused to see a medical doctor for fear that it could be cancer. Mother said he had developed a phobia about cancer after several of his colleagues went into the hospital and never came out again. Father's position was that if he had cancer, he didn't want to know. Even the word was banned in our house; it became "that disease."

"What are you afraid of?" I asked after his coughing brought an abrupt end to our lunch. "So what if you have cancer? Isn't it good to find out sooner rather than later, so you can get treatment?" Father's face went red and he started to shake and he asked me to stop. I had been mean, and I regretted my words. He set down his bowl and left the house, presumably to think, because he later asked me to find him a reliable doctor. I switched my classes with another teacher and took him to the hospital.

Pneumonia was the initial diagnosis and he was relieved. He was given a course of antibiotics. I was relieved too and went back to school. A week later, his condition hadn't improved and I took him back to the hospital. Further tests revealed cancer cells in his lungs. I took him to three different hospitals, desperately hoping the first diagnosis had been a mistake. The results were the same, as was the prognosis—advanced stage, no point in surgery. Localized chemotherapy might put off the inevitable, but it would not be pleasant. We tried to hide the diagnosis from him, but he learned the truth when he overheard the doctor discussing his case with an intern. Father's whole world crumbled around him. Within weeks, his face took on a grayish hue and he grew terribly thin from the chemo. I couldn't bear to see him suffer and turned to nontraditional medicine in hope of finding a cure, taking overnight trains here and there to consult with herbal doctors, after which we boiled herbs and mixed powders. We transferred Father to a more prestigious hospital in the hope of finding better doctors. We tried everything that friends suggested or had heard was effective. Mother even wrapped a toad in white linen and placed it over his lungs—the toad was supposed to suck the poison from his lungs. I had a morbid fear of toads and, under any other circumstance, would have thought the idea idiotic. Father's health did not improve. Looking at photos of me from that time, I appear thin, skeletal. I forgot to eat and barely slept. At some point, my university gave me an award for "model teacher," but I didn't hear them call on me to stand as I had fallen asleep.

Father's absence made Grandma anxious and she clutched my hands the moment I returned from the hospital, asking if Father was still alive. Five minutes later, she would clutch my hands and repeat the question, as if I had just come home and not already carefully told her what I thought she should know.

In September, it was time for me to begin my graduate studies in Shanghai. I thought I should stay because the doctors did not sound at all confident about Father's prognosis, but he told me to go. "Your future is more important," he said. "Your success will help with the fortunes of our family." He snuck home the night I left to see me off. That night he also gave Mother the key to the desk drawer where he kept all his savings and papers.

It was an exciting time to be in journalism. The media was attempting to move away from its traditional role as the Party's mouthpiece to that of watchdog. Our university invited an

Australian journalist to teach my class and we had speakers from well-known newspapers run by reformists. But I couldn't focus. Father's illness weighed heavily on my mind. I stayed in contact as best I could, monitoring the progress of this or that course of treatment, but the prognosis never changed.

One night, I woke up from a nightmare about losing a tooth, which my dorm mate suggested signified death in the family. His interpretation kept me awake all night long. I called Father the next morning and he sounded fine. He was trying more alternative therapies. Our conversation was cut short by the arrival of a group of Christians who wanted to pray for his recovery. He said Mother had asked them over. Many of the old women in the neighborhood had begun attending church services after the Party relaxed its restrictions on religion. "But you're a Communist," I teased. "Didn't Karl Marx say religion is spiritual opium to fool the people?" He replied, "If it helps me recover, I'm willing to take opium."

Three days later, a telegram was handed to me in the middle of an international conference—HURRY HOME. YOUR FATHER IS DYING. I caught the overnight train and was met at the station by a friend of Father's, who had borrowed the company jeep. He said that Father's heart had been weak since the previous day and that Father had begged the doctors to keep him alive until I arrived, glancing at the clock every few minutes and asking, "Is he here yet?" We drove fast, swerving in and out of traffic. I was breathless when I reached the ICU. Father was on oxygen. Numerous tubes ran into and out of his emaciated body. His hair was a dull, lank gray, long and unkempt. He recognized me and, as I sat beside him, he gasped through his oxygen mask. "The treatment doesn't work. See if your friends can find a better hospital." Those were his last words. Three hours later, he was in a coma. The doctor said that Father might struggle on for another day or two, but it was unlikely he would regain consciousness. He asked whether I would consent to withdrawing treatment rather than prolonging his suffering. Thinking how desperately Father wanted to live until he saw me, I struggled and waited for another day, hoping for a miracle to happen. As I sat down by him and saw his laborious breathing, I decided to take up the doctor's offer. I didn't tell Mother of my decision, but warned her that Father would probably pass soon, maybe the following morning. "We must gather the family to see him off," she said. "It is unlucky for a person to leave alone." She talked as if we were sending Father on a trip to Beijing, and I became irritated by her talk of ritual and tradition. Mostly, I did not want a bunch of relatives crying and howling by his bed. I sent her home to make her preparations. My brother-in-law stayed and joined me in my vigil. After the doctor unplugged the tubes, I was racked with guilt until, overwhelmed by my thoughts, I sought out the doctor and pleaded with him to keep trying. But it was already too late; Father's breathing quickened, his body twitched and fell still, the muscles of his face relaxed into the calmness of untroubled sleep.

Father passed away on October 31, 1988, which I later found out was Halloween in America. As I wiped his cold, naked body clean, I sobbed. My brother-in-law was with me and pulled me aside and reminded me that it was taboo to shed tears on the body of a loved one, saying, "If he carries your tears to the other world, sadness will accompany him." I was not a villager and deferred to his greater knowledge of tradition. Regaining my composure, we dressed him in the new clothes Mother had bought for him, gray trousers and a simple navy blue Mao jacket, which was appropriate for a Party member. To prevent us from taking his body home, two male nurses were notified immediately to take Father's body to the hospital morgue from where we could collect it when arrangements had been made for his cremation. I stood in a daze, watching them push the stretcher toward the elevator door, the sound of the squeaking wheels echoing in the long, empty corridor. "He doesn't want to go, he's struggling to stay," my brother-in-law murmured.

Grandma was sitting on the couch, waiting for me when I got home the next morning. My siblings were out notifying relatives. Mother was being consoled at a neighbor's house. Grandma had not been told that Father was dead, but she was having one of her lucid moments and knew something was seriously amiss. I did not want to be the one to tell her and asked a relative to come take her so we could plan Father's wake. She moaned and struggled as we carried her out to a flatbed tricycle and peddled through the busy streets. At the relative's house, she grabbed at my hands like a fearful child and begged me not to leave. There is a saying in China, and I think the sentiment is universal if in different words: "It is tragic for the gray-haired to send off the dark-haired." I shared her grief, but I felt resentment too, because of the way she had manipulated him into spending the better part of his life planning her funeral and it sucked him dry until there was nothing left but his own corpse.

On reflection, I am appalled at how badly I behaved after Father's death. I was now the head of the family and determined, as if to punish him for his obsession with tradition, to strip his funeral of all ritual. "He lived like a model Communist Party member," I said, "and so, according to instructions from the Party, we should proceed to Sanzhao Crematorium and be done with it." I knew I was being unreasonable, but I was angry. Mother ignored me. "The Party allows people to have traditional wakes and funerals, as long as the deceased is cremated," she said, and she glared at me. "Your Father would want this. I know him."

Relatives and neighbors argued over whether Xi'an or Henan custom should be followed for the wake and I reasserted my authority and declared that, as a Xi'an native myself, we would follow local tradition. The apartment was stripped of all decoration, including Grandma's antique mirror and a poster of a movie star my sister had put up in the living room, and all the furniture was draped in black. A grainy photograph of Father was placed on a table, with an incense burner and five small plates of fruit and cookies around it. In the picture, which had been taken for his upcoming retirement, his hair looked untidy and his eyes sad, as if he had already foreseen his fate. Someone brought white linen shirts for me and my siblings. I refused to wear mine, but agreed to a long white headband. Relatives and friends came, some sobbing or wailing, and bowed before his portrait and burned a slip of coarse yellow paper in an urn, a symbolic offering to the next world.

The Party secretary of Father's company came in, followed by the trade-union chairman. They delivered a big wreath and shook hands with everyone, saying that Father was a good man and a model Party member. I nodded through my cynicism. I was supposed to negotiate with the Party secretary to conclude any unfinished business of Father's, which included the transfer of my brother from a small textile cooperative to Father's state-run company. "You are the oldest son," Mother said when I tried to get out of the duty. "With your father gone, you will be the one to take care of your siblings." This was difficult for me—at age twenty-four, I did not feel prepared for such a big responsibility and when it came time to speak, all our rehearsal was for nothing. I could only stammer, as I had when I was a child. Mother took over and succeeded in settling Father's affairs to our advantage. Before the company representatives left, the trade-union chairman requested I say a few words after the Party secretary's eulogy. As Mother nodded vigorously in agreement, my mind went blank.

More than two hundred people came to Father's wake, and wreaths filled the first-floor corridor and spilled outside. "Your father was a good man, *laoshi*, a filial son." Every visitor began with those words. *Laoshi* loosely translates as "genuine and honest." Mother had often called Father *laoshi*, but as is typical of so much in Chinese, words have many meanings; when she said *laoshi*, it meant "weak and incompetent."

I didn't know what to think of Father. I needed to say something, but the words wouldn't come to me. I had written self-criticisms for classmates, drafted applications for Party membership, penned important speeches for others to deliver. I knew all the political jargon, the right combinations of words that expressed deep regret without sounding insincere or making promises that sounded empty. I could make Party members sound as though Communism had taken root in their very being. For Father, I had nothing. I could blame years of Communist indoctrination for inhibiting the free expression of personal feelings. But I think it was the arrogance of youth. I couldn't deliver a talk without feeling disdainful for what I considered the trivial life Father had led and without offending the Communist Party which he had faithfully served.

For most of his life, Father worked without complaint as a warehouse manager, taking pride in being recognized as a model Communist by his company and as a filial son by his neighbors. He married Mother at twenty-eight and raised four children, doing his part to revive the Huang line that was almost wiped out by disease, flood, and war. As the only surviving child, Father took care of Grandma all his life. For years, he was thankful for a stable life untouched by the worst of the political turmoil of his times. But for all his loyalty to the Party, when China was freed from the radical ideological control of Chairman Mao and began slowly to prosper, he and millions of workers, the vanguard of the proletariat who underwrote Communist China, were left behind, confused and disillusioned. He died because his lungs had been scarred by years of exposure to industrial pollutants, his heart broken by the unrealized 6.5-yuan promotion and the depth of corruption that had twisted the ideals of the Party he had supported.

I struggled with the speech, hoping that the bitterness would evaporate and inspiration would hit me at the last minute.

The night before the cremation, I was supposed to carry Father's picture and lead my siblings around the neighborhood, chanting and wailing to call his soul back for a final "reunion" before sending him off to the other world, which I did, but only under protest. At the main crossroads, a relative chalked a circle on the footpath and placed within it stacks of fake money that he set alight while calling Father's name. "Come back, Zhiyou, your children are here to greet you. We'll see you off tomorrow morning. Have a peaceful trip. Don't worry about your mother and your children. They will be well taken care of." As the flames danced in the air and the autumn wind scattered the ashes, the relative turned to me and said excitedly, "Look at the flames. Your father is here to collect the gifts." I nodded, but as the crowd began another round of wailing, I wanted to laugh at all this absurd ritual. Fortunately I did not have to carry a bamboo pole with a long strip of white paper tied to it at the procession, which I dreaded doing as a child. For the cremation itself, I was handed the urn containing the ashes of all those yellow slips of paper burned during the wake. I was supposed to smash the urn when the procession reached the crossroads. The urn symbolized the body that had contained Father's spirit in this life; breaking it would liberate him so he could be reincarnated. The urn broke into many small pieces.

At the crematorium, I was surprised by the size of the turn-out; so many friends and colleagues had come. Father's body was inside a glass case on the podium. When he was alive, I had never seen his face look so peaceful. An uncle of mine had shaved his beard that morning before we moved him from the morgue but had missed a couple of spots on his left cheek. When the loud-speakers blaring Communist funeral music fell silent, the trade-union chairman asked everyone to bow three times to Father's body and the Party secretary read from a sheet of paper: "While many people became distracted at work and focused their energy on outside opportunities to make themselves rich, Comrade Huang remained dedicated and found ways for the company to save money . . ." And so on. His speech was long, but it seemed to take but a moment to deliver and then it was my turn to speak. I panicked, nothing came to my mind. A good friend nudged me and whispered, "Just bow and say 'thank you,'" which I did and kept my eyes on the floor as I walked back from the podium, unable to face the crowd. There was a long silence before the trade-union chairman stepped in and announced, "Let's line up and pay last tribute to Comrade Huang."

Mother never allowed me to forget my shame. She would tell me about every funeral she attended: how this eldest son—and she'd pointedly remark that he had never attended university—told stories about his deceased father that made everyone cry; or how a young woman had sung her father's favorite operatic aria and there was not a dry eye to be seen. Making people cry was her gold standard for a good eulogy. I would roll my eyes in contempt at her tactics, the knife of guilt plunged deep into in my heart.

One of Mother's cousins brought two bottles of liquor and two cartons of cigarettes to bribe the crematorium workers to make sure they emptied the furnace without mixing Father's ashes with those of others, as was common in Xi'an. We placed the remains in a wooden cinerary urn in the shape of an ancient palace. A young female custodian in charge of storage pointed at the rows of beehivelike wooden shelves and picked a niche on the bottom shelf, saying, "It's good to place it lower. It will make it easier for your father to step out and visit you." She was so earnest and spoke with such seriousness that I wanted to laugh, but her words were comforting.

As I opened Father's drawer at home and sorted through his papers, I made a pile of the considerable correspondence relating to Grandma's funeral, looking for a clue that might lead me to understand why he had become so obsessed about something his mother would never know had happened. How futile his efforts had been, this superstitious belief that he could somehow reunite Grandma and Grandpa and harness the blessings of our ancestors—where lay the blessing in his premature death?

I asked Mother if she had instructions from Father about Grandma's burial. She shook her head. Grandma's funeral never came up in his final days. "Like your Grandma, Father didn't want to talk about death," Mother said. "He didn't even mention Grandma." Mother recalled that Father missed home and was very concerned about Grandma when he was first hospitalized. He would walk Mother to the entrance like a little boy and longed to come home with her. Against the doctor's advice, my sister arranged for a company car to bring Father home for a weekend. As Father rested up, he saw Grandma wobble around in her demented state and grab the food that friends had brought over as if nobody had been present. Father cried, saddened by Grandma's dementia and his own helplessness. The next morning, he asked to be sent back to the hospital and never mentioned going home again. Before his death, Father mentioned Grandma one more time, saying his mother's karma was too strong. "I think your father couldn't understand why cancer would hit him so early. I guess he resented the fact that Grandma had controlled his whole life and after everything he had done, she would outlive him."

When a company official visited Mother after the funeral to ask if there was anything the family needed, Mother told him about Father's wish that Grandma be returned to Henan after she died for a traditional burial. Would the company help transport the coffin? The official thought for a moment and, presumably content that the burial would take place in another province and was beyond the company's jurisdiction, said, "That shouldn't be a problem." He was probably relieved that the company got off so lightly.

Grandma did not recognize me when I went to fetch her after the funeral. She didn't seem to recognize anyone, nor did she seem familiar with her surroundings. An elderly neighbor told me that Father must have taken her soul with him. Grandma's care was left to Mother and my sisters. Father's death softened Mother's attitude toward Grandma; my sister said she had heard Mother whisper to Father's body during the funeral that she would continue to take care of his mother and give her a proper send-off.

As eldest son, I felt responsible for ensuring that Father's wishes be carried out, and the weight of that responsibility spilled over to my dreams, in which Father became a regular visitor. I started to pay attention to what they might mean in the real world. One of those vivid dreams started when Father came in to our house and attempted to take Grandma away. I grabbed Grandma's legs, begging Father to drop her. "Let me take care of her," I screamed. Father paused for a few seconds and said, "Okay, I will let you have her for one year." Without hesitation, Mother offered her interpretation: "Your father will be back to get her in a year."

17.

REVOLUTION

Until 1989, the Qingming Festival in April meant little to us. It is the day when families attend to the tombs and graves of the dead, a venerable and deeply felt practice that even the Party had made no serious attempt to challenge. Father's passing had imbued the day with new significance. Mother planned a small ceremony at a memorial park near the crematorium. As it was the first time our family had observed the ritual, I took the long train ride home, motivated by the desire to see Grandma rather than by any significant loyalty to Father's memory.

My thoughts were about death and its significance as I returned to Shanghai on April 15, which is perhaps why I listened so intently to the radio broadcasts announcing that former Communist Party General Secretary Hu Yaobang had died of a heart attack. I was no fan of Hu's overexuberant manners, and I was sympathetic to Father's distress when Hu abruptly invited three thousand young Japanese to visit China in a gesture of goodwill and friendship. The presence of so many Japanese triggered bitter memories of the Chinese suffering at the hands of the Japanese invaders during World War II. Beijing may have wanted rapprochement with Tokyo, but the Party propaganda machine still had a lot to do to convince the country to forget the consequences of Japanese imperialism.

On the Fudan campus, Hu was seen as a reformist leader who, unlike many of his conservative rivals, advocated a more open government with an independent judiciary and an independent press. That caught my attention; at the time I was wrestling with the meaning and significance of an independent press in a country as large and complicated as China, where individual freedoms were nonexistent. More important, I was told by my fellow students that Hu was free of the taint of corruption and had wanted concerted efforts to rein in inflation, which many attributed to speculation and profiteering by the children of Party officials. The information changed my view of Hu. Personally, I felt very concerned about the direction of the economic reforms.

At that time, China was moving deeper into its economic transition, but runaway inflation sent waves of panic across the country. Rice, flour, and even big electrical appliances became scarce as people turned their increasingly worthless paper money into tangible assets. When goods ran out and prices soared higher, the children and relatives of senior Party officials were blamed for abusing their power and manipulating the marketplace. "All the money we saved over the past twenty years for Grandma's funeral is probably not enough to buy a color TV now," said Father, when he was in the hospital. He sighed a long sigh, one of futility and helplessness. It is a sigh etched in my mind. Memory of Father's reaction compelled me to join the demonstrations.

There was revolution in the air in the weeks following Hu's death, and the government was unprepared for the protest movement that coalesced in cities around the country. At Fudan University, students stopped attending classes, and demonstrations and rallies, many seemingly spontaneous, brought daily life to a standstill. From my perch on a high window overlooking the crowds in downtown Shanghai, it looked and felt like a revolution, and I was gripped with the urge to join those at the front, but Father's words sounded clearly in my head: "Don't be a show-off; the gun will shoot the head of the flock." I refrained, even though part of me could not help feeling disappointed at my cowardice. In May, a graduate student in the law department came to me with a white headband and asked me to join a hunger strike. He had grown up in Xi'an's rural hinterland and had never struck me as a firebrand. I declined. When I brought him water and a blanket out of concern for his health and safety, I could not find him among the hunger strikers. That evening, I spotted him at the student cafeteria. "I was so hungry. I'm not going to lose my health for those bastards in the government." He was back among the hunger strikers the next morning. Though there were clearly many issues that needed to be addressed, ordinary people gradually lost interest as the government in Shanghai scared them with scenarios of food supply interruptions if chaos occurred. Students like me continued to draw inspiration from the experiences of former Red Guards, who described traveling all over the country in the name of spreading the Revolution. I got caught up in the excitement and traveled to Beijing, where the focus was the vast Tiananmen Square, which was filled with people from out of town since most of the local students were experiencing "protest fatigue" after camping out for nearly a month and had returned to campus. I stayed with friends and heard about all the inside bickering within the student leadership ranks. Nobody seemed to have a clear direction. Disillusioned, I left Beijing on June 1 and returned to Shanghai with the idea that we might be able to generate new momentum by following Chairman Mao's path and mobilizing workers on strike.

As children, we were fed stories about how much the army loved the people and how much the Party cared for us. Though we expected the government to retaliate, and were confused about why it had not done so, none of us had foreseen the events of June 4, 1989, when the People's Liberation Army opened fire on the people it was supposed to protect. News of the crackdown reached Shanghai. We were in shock. Father used to describe me as "a young cub who hasn't tasted the fear of death." That was exactly true. We took to the streets carrying lanterns to symbolize the darkness into which China had been plunged. I wore a white headband and we held banners denouncing the Communist Party's brutality. Bus drivers abandoned their vehicles, blocking roads to disrupt the advance of any military forces that might be sent into Shanghai. Since the Party imposed a news blackout for the next three days, ordinary citizens had no idea that many students and residents in Beijing had been killed by government troops. My classmates and I turned to our portable shortwave radios and learned from the BBC and Voice of America what had truly happened in Beijing. One of my teachers, an Australian, gave me a copy of Hong Kong's English-language newspaper, which carried pictures of wounded protesters soaked in blood on the streets of Beijing, and we made copies and papered the streets around the university to expose the government brutality. I climbed atop a bus and called on workers to strike. I was aware I might later be punished for my actions, but nothing happened. Perhaps no one heard me, perhaps no one thought my actions serious enough to bother reporting. I was not among the "counterrevolutionaries" rounded up in mid-June as the government launched its nationwide crackdown on dissent. Two organizers from my department were arrested. Fearing that I could be a target if I stayed, I hid a cache of pictures and pamphlets and left the city to visit a friend in the mountainous Shaanxi region, traveling by boat and bus to avoid police patrolling the trains. I thought I was safe when, at the train station where I was supposed to meet my friend, I was stopped by uniformed railway police, who seized my luggage and marched me to a nearby office. My legs were shaking; it was hard to breathe; and I was worried I might pee my pants. I heard loud laughter—it was my friend; the uniformed police were students of his and they were all amused at the success of their little joke. "I thought you were a tough revolutionary," he said. "I guess I was wrong."

I returned to Xi'an in July and spent the summer in a deep funk. I met with a friend who was among the protesters in Beijing when the massacre took place. He and other students had hurled stones and bottles in their futile attempt to block the rumbling tanks near Xidan, a busy shopping district in the city. Quite unexpectedly, some soldiers appeared from a side street on their left and started shooting at them. My friend immediately scrambled into an alley and cowered under a large garbage bin, but a flying bullet hit a young man running behind him; his stomach oozed blood. Fortunately, he and several passersby found a bicycle and wheeled the young man to a nearby hospital, where dozens of other wounded residents were being treated. He did not know if the young man lived or died. For days, my friend had problems sleeping. When I asked about the killings in Tiananmen Square, he did acknowledge that the government was technically correct in claiming that no students were killed in the square when the troops moved in, but he estimated that five to six hundred people were gunned down elsewhere in the city, disputing the exaggerated assertions by the Western media and some of the student leaders who had escaped to the West that "tens of thousands of people had died in Tiananmen Square and in other parts of Beijing."

Meanwhile, as part of the government's efforts to cover up the bloody suppression, the media launched a nationwide propaganda campaign. On television, shots of the burned corpses of soldiers and the debris of damaged trucks and tanks were replayed again and again as evidence against those "hooligans and counterrevolutionaries." On the streets of Xi'an, loudspeaker trucks

broadcast the Party's latest condemnation of the student leaders who wanted only to cause unrest in China. The propaganda
worked. Neighbors and friends, who had been the students'
enthusiastic supporters, began to blame us for disrupting the stability of the country. Even my uncle, who had suffered severe
beatings during the Cultural Revolution, embraced the Party's
decision. "You students were no better than the Red Guards," he
lectured. "It was necessary to put down the movement. Otherwise you would have plunged the country into chaos!" It felt like
the start of another Mao era. I was angry and I was disappointed.
I wrote to an American professor I had met in Shanghai a year
before, expressing my desire to leave the country and escape the
oppressive political environment. Occasionally, I began practicing meditation, fantasizing about spending the rest of my life in a
monastery, free from worldly concerns. But Grandma and memories of Father kept me going and as her health deteriorated, I
had little time to think about my future.

We had feared the worst when Grandma woke the house
with a burst of activity. She seemed lucid, recognized me, asked
where Father was, and announced: "I'm going to cook for you.
Your mother was always so mean to your father. I'm going to
show her how to make noodles." She had grabbed a cutting board
and a knife before we could stop her, but my brother and I managed to get her back to her room, though she put up a struggle
and tossed and turned for half an hour before she exhausted her
strength and fell into a deep sleep. When I checked on her the
next morning, she had no idea who I was and had barely enough
strength to use the chamber pot. Dr. Gao said that sudden bursts

of energy meant she would soon be dead, but again she survived the summer. Each morning, when I woke up, she was there sitting on her bed, blubbering senselessly to herself. I tended to her needs, feeding and bathing her, washing her clothes, cleaning up after her incontinence. I refused to give up, and even as she was struck with fever and was hooked up to IV drips by a friend from the hospital, I rubbed alcohol on her forehead and her back in an attempt to make her comfortable.

Mother dismissed my effort as pointless. "You are only prolonging Grandma's suffering," she argued. "We should let her go." I ignored her.

When the fall semester started and it was time for me to return to Shanghai, Mother insisted I go. "It's critical you go back to clarify your role in the student movement," she said, and drew on her experiences during the Cultural Revolution. "If you are not there, others could dump all sorts of crimes on you and you will not be able to defend yourself." Reluctantly, I left Grandma to Mother's care and departed for Shanghai.

The government continued to condemn the "counterrevolutionary riots" through editorials in the *People's Daily*, and more people were arrested. Our class closed ranks and we protected one another. We were simply ordinary participants and had not engaged in any radical activity. Our teacher vouched for us. We wrote self-criticisms and that, it seemed, was that. We were not what many in the West called "prodemocracy" fighters. We were young and passionate, certainly, but we got involved in the protest movement for the excitement. We had no deep philosophical convictions. For my generation, the brutal crackdown was a rite of passage. Our belief system, based as it was on years of brain-washing, collapsed. We woke up from the illusion that we could change China from within the Communist system. It is not surprising that some of us have become fearless democracy activists. The extensive coverage of the massacre by the western media was good for the Chinese government too, because it realized it could not simply shut out the world and behave as if its actions had no consequences.

Despite my busy schedule at school, Grandma was never far from my mind. November 30, 1989, was a Wednesday. I was unable to concentrate on my classes. Thoughts of Grandma kept popping into my head; they were happy thoughts. I skipped the afternoon political study session and went downtown to make a long distance call to my sister's office. A stranger answered her phone: "Your sister is home today. Your grandma has died."

Surprised by my call, Mother dissuaded me from coming home for the funeral. It would be unwise to leave Shanghai at such a politically sensitive time, she counseled. She put two of Father's friends on the phone and they said much the same thing. Mother said that Grandma had a peaceful death and that my brother and sisters were there when she died. She had lived to eighty-seven, a good age.

For more than a decade, my family had prepared for that dreadful moment. Father spent the better part of his life working on the funeral, meticulously planning every stage, including a small secret open-casket wake inside our house for relatives, the transportation of Grandma's body to Henan, and the organization of a traditional procession outside Grandma's native village.

He had personally designated pallbearers, drivers, grave diggers, and a host whose job was to deliver gifts to the village officials and smooth the way for Grandma's burial. Mother had purchased a bolt of white linen back in the early 1980s for our mourning costumes. Father specifically included me in every phase of the preparations, claiming frequently that the son and eldest grandson were key players driving the funeral. Sadly, none of us was there.

Ironically, Mother, who had constantly been accused by Grandma of sabotaging her burial, was left to take charge. Mother decided that, with Father gone and me away, it would be too difficult to get Grandma all the way back to Henan. We could wait until another time, she told me on the phone. I paused. I began to feel sorry for Grandma. For years, Mother claimed that if she had her way, she would bury or cremate Grandma in Xi'an. She certainly triumphed over Grandma. Being hundreds of miles away from home, I felt powerless to change the arrangement. Nonetheless, I was relieved that Mother honored part of Father's promise by granting Grandma a proper burial in a plot of land that my brother-in-law had secured in his native village outside the city.

To head off any potential gossip that, given the past acrimony, she had cut corners, Mother delegated her duties to an uncle on Father's side of the family. A tent went up outside our building. The coffin was retrieved from the warehouse. Friends arrived to help Mother dress Grandma in the outfit that had been made for her fifteen years earlier. A steady stream of people came to pay homage. Mother was asked for token gifts—a piece of Grandma's quilt or a hairpin—so people could pass on some of her luck and longevity to their children. Two strips of blue cloth from one of Grandma's old shirts were set aside for my brother and me.

The funeral was deliberately small; the police had been stopping large processions and sending them straight to the crematorium.

At four o'clock in the morning, three vans and a truck arrived amid pouring rain. The coffin was loaded onto the truck. Mourners quietly boarded the vans without the usual wailing and urn-smashing ritual. The little convoy made good time on the empty streets and a policeman uncle asked the drivers to circle the landmark bell tower in the city center to give Grandma one last look at Xi'an, her home for half a century. The journey took less than two hours and the rain stopped as Grandma was laid to rest in a small cemetery near an abandoned brick factory three miles south of the city. My sister recalls that when a relative tried to hammer nails in the coffin, it took him several tries before he could drive them in. "Grandma doesn't want to leave because her son and favorite grandson are not here to see her off," he said to everyone.

Father joined Grandma. The urn containing Father's ashes, retrieved earlier from its niche in the crematorium, was buried separately near the bottom left corner of Grandma's coffin. Father's location, at the feet of his mother, meant the son would always be at his mother's service.

For months I had problems concentrating at school. I felt numb, only dully aware of my surroundings. In senior high school, a friend of mine lost her mother and an elder sister to cancer within six months of each other. I used to visit them every week at the hospital. It was not all altruistic. Misguided teenager that I was, I wanted to wallow in the Shakespearean glamour of her tragedy, and I welcomed the exciting possibilities of reinventing a life without one's nagging parents. In comparison, I lamented my own life, boring and devoid of any drama—Grandma seemed to live forever and my parents were still in their prime. I didn't know fate could be so brutal. When death struck my family, I cursed my youthful hubris. The feeling of loss and emptiness was acute and sharp, like the cutting of a kite string, as if my connection with home had simply ceased to exist.

I did not speak to Mother. I did not speak to my siblings. During winter break, I went back to Xi'an and sat in Grandma's room. It was apparent that Mother had already moved on. Grandma's clothes, the bamboo basket that she had used to store all my treats, her walking stick, and her chamber pot were all gone. The mattress that I had bought for Grandma was now covered with a brand-new sheet. In fact, Mother cleaned out the room so thoroughly that I could not find a single thing that was distinctively Grandma's. I was very tempted to vent my displeasure with what Mother had done, but considering it was my first day at home, I suppressed my urge.

Father taught me that the dead never abandon the living; the spirits communicate their wishes through dreams. My atheist Communist upbringing and my education in science made me instinctively reject such beliefs as superstitious, even idiotic. But now I found them soothing. That night, I slept on Grandma's bed, hoping she might come to me in my dreams and we could talk some more. She didn't.

The next day, Mother accompanied me on my first visit to Grandma's tomb, which was in the shape of a small pyramid. We lit some stacks of fake money. "Your grandson is back," Mother whispered. "Use the money to buy something nice for yourself."

As smoke spiraled into the gray winter sky, Mother swept the ashes while trying to justify her decision. "I don't think Grandma would mind being close to her grandchildren. Now that she is close by, we can easily hop on a bus and pay tribute to her during holidays." Seeing that I didn't answer, she said, "Oh, well, if you don't like it, you can still move Grandma back to her hometown after the traditional three-year mourning period." I wasn't sure. Like she said, Grandma might be happy here, with Father at her side.

In January of 1990, I spent my first Lunar New Year without Father and Grandma. On New Year's Day, I suddenly found myself without anything to do. I used to hate going with Father on those visits to uncles and aunties who had promised to help with Grandma's funeral. Now I wished that Father was here to take me, even though it meant that we had to stay out late and miss the New Year's concert on TV.

18.

INDEPENDENCE

Mother was alone now. My sisters had married. My brother was busy with his girlfriend and I was busy with my studies in Shanghai. As the eldest son, my foremost Confucian obligation was to care for my mother, but I had my career to think about and did not intend to move back to Xi'an, where Mother planned to spend the rest of her life. In addition, following Grandma's death, I still felt alienated from Mother. I think nothing scared me more than the thought of following Father's path and having Mother by my side for the rest of her life and even after death. "Don't worry, I'm not your Grandma," she reassured me. "I have my pension and I have my friends. I'm not going to be a burden to any of you." She was a fiercely independent woman, but I still felt guilty, probably because of how disappointed I imagined Father would be after the years he had spent trying to instill in me a sense of filial obligation.

At the end of 1989, thanks to the American professor, I was accepted to a graduate program at a university in Illinois. After camping out in front of the American consulate in Shanghai for a whole night, I received my visa from a journalist-turned-consul, who was thrilled that I intended to pursue journalism in a free country. When it was time to tell Mother about my planned trip to America in February 1990, I didn't know if she would allow me to leave. But she did.

Barely a year after I arrived in the United States, I received a rushed telephone call from my younger sister. "Mother has a boyfriend," she said. I could almost hear her calculating the astronomical cost of the call down to the second in those days before the Internet. "It's Uncle Ma," she said. "I'll write more in a letter." Then she hung up.

Uncle Ma was an apprentice with Father in the early 1950s and, having grown up in the same province, they were "sworn brothers," but over the years their friendship cooled. He had an important position inside the city government, and Father used to call him a snob and an opportunist. We heard that Uncle Ma had divorced, married again, and lost his new wife to cancer. He came to Father's funeral and began stopping by now and then to inquire after Grandma's health, but I was unaware of any interest on Mother's part because she would try to avoid him during such visits, leaving me to entertain Uncle Ma while she dashed off on some forgotten errand. "A widow could easily become the target of vicious gossip," she said. I thought she was being "feudalistic."

My older sister discovered the truth when she went to visit Mother at the hospital after a minor surgery and found her bed empty. The nurse said a man had taken her home. My sister called my brother, who said Mother wasn't there. She phoned around; someone suggested that she try Uncle Ma. "I'm taking care of her here for a couple of days," he said, in what my sister remarked was "measured casualness." There was an uproar among the children of both families.

"Father is turning in his grave," my older sister said to Mother. "For a person your age, it's shameless." That was too much for Mother; tough as she was, she cried. My sister regretted her words but not her opposition to the relationship so soon after Father's death. Uncle Ma's children thought Mother was after their father's money and refused to talk to her, let alone acknowledge her.

Nowadays, the government openly applauds the union of a widow and a widower as practical, and Mother's moving in with Uncle Ma would cause scarcely a ripple in an increasingly tolerant China. In 1990 it was still scandalous—probably not enough for Mother to be vilified at a Mao-era public denunciation meeting for being a "broken shoe"—a morally loose woman—but it was juicy fodder for neighborhood gossips.

Women face a paradox in China. Chairman Mao said, "Women hold up half the sky." They worked side by side with men in the factories and fields, and Mao called for the elimination of traditional moral values that contributed to inequality, but Confucianism has deep roots in China and it often was taken to extremes. I remember that a young married couple was caught kissing in a secluded corner of a Xi'an park in the late 1970s. Security guards detained them, charged them with lewd conduct, and notified their companies before releasing them. Change came, but it arrived slowly. In 1983, after China had opened up to the West, a well-known actor was sentenced to four years in prison after neighbors reported that he had attended a private dance party at a friend's home and had engaged in premarital sex with a young woman. In my faculty at Fudan University, our political counselor was tipped off that a sophomore was sneaking his girlfriend into his dorm when his roommates were out at the movies. The counselor caught them and both students were publicly denounced at our monthly all-student meeting; after graduation, they were assigned jobs in remote locations far from each other.

Things changed fast. By the time I left for the United States in 1990, my brother's girlfriend frequently stayed overnight at our house and the neighbors found nothing in their lifestyle worth gossiping about. Young people did little that surprised them, but for Mother's generation, it was as if time had stood still. The neighborhood wasn't short of widows or widowers, but no one remarried, let alone got divorced.

Apparently Mother and Uncle Ma began seeing each other soon after Father's death. Mother had started a small grocery store in our building. She craved companionship. Although she was a dutiful member of the neighborhood sewing group that made quilts for brides-to-be, Mother, as a widow, was forbidden to touch bridal gifts for fear of tainting their future luck.

Uncle Ma's presence was comforting to Mother. My younger sister reported that Mother began to pay attention to her looks and would wear the nice clothes that Uncle Ma had bought her. Unlike Father, Uncle Ma was a good cook. He would come in to help with her business and do household chores. "We both felt that we had done enough for you children," Mother told me. "We deserve to have our own life." They began to go out together in public and were soon married without ceremony, living sometimes in his house, sometimes in ours. During holidays, she would stay at Uncle Ma's house to prepare a feast for his four children, hoping they would gradually change their minds about her. Then, feeling guilty that she had done nothing for her own children, she rushed home to cook for my siblings.

"Nobody has treated me with such tenderness and care," Mother told me. "He prepares breakfast before I get up and buys me clothes." Her remarks didn't shock me. Did she ever love Father, or did Father ever love her? "In my generation, we were not like Westerners and we didn't say 'I love you' every day. We just took care of each other and our family." It was true, and by that measure, I suppose they loved each other in a Chinese way. However, when I probed further about their relationship, she said, "Your father was a filial son and an attentive parent, but he was a lousy husband, even though he was getting better in the last decade of his life."

Mother said she had long realized that she would never wrestle Father away from Grandma and found it easier not to fight it in the later years, which is not to say that they didn't argue when it came to Grandma as well as his meddling in matters of money.

Did she ever think of leaving Father in the years when Grandma's funeral seemed to consume all of his attention? Was she faithful to him? I recall a man whom we referred to as Uncle Wang. At the age of five, I visited Mother at work and noticed that Uncle Wang met up with her every evening. Was he her lover? No. She blushed at the thought. "He was merely a good friend." During her worst fights with Father, divorce never even crossed her mind.

When I had thought it all through, I was happy for Mother. Uncle Ma was probably her first true love and I supported their marriage. My siblings did not, and said I was too westernized, that I had forgotten what life was like in China. The early days of her second marriage were certainly difficult. The presence of a new man in our house raised many eyebrows. Relatives and neighbors, even Mother's older sister, measured her against Grandma, who was a virtuous traditional woman in their eyes for remaining a widow all her life. Father's niece and aunt stopped visiting. Mother said she knew people talked behind her back, but she walked with her head high. "She chose to give up her life for your father. I want to live my own life."

The strong opposition from my younger brother caused Mother the most distress. Following Father's death, he was transferred to Father's company, so all the gossip about Mother and Uncle Ma reached his ears. He felt humiliated. He constantly argued with Mother, accusing her of ruining the family name—this when he had a live-in girlfriend. He began drinking heavily, on at least one occasion making a scene at work. My younger sister was called to come get him and, in his ramblings, he vowed,

"I'm kicking her out of my life." Mother endured all this without comment.

Little by little, relatives accepted her decision and after their initial outrage, my brother and sisters gradually reconciled with Mother. Gossips found other targets. She never got a red certificate, but Mother's little act of defiance against convention started a small revolution as other widows and widowers began stepping out of their comfort zone and discreetly asking for her advice on dating.

In 1992, Mother received a phone call from her half brother in Henan. Gong-gong had been killed in a traffic accident. She and Aunt Xiuying rushed home to plan their father's funeral. They also insisted that Po-po, their biological mother, be buried alongside Gong-gong. Mother, who had kept quiet on the issue all her life, became vocal and threatened to take Gong-gong's body hostage if their request was not met. Their half brothers and sisters consented. Mother and Aunt Xiuying bought a small coffin, which contained a wooden marker with Po-po's name on it and three sets of *shou-yi*. They burned incense, cried, and wailed to summon the spirit of their mother, whose looks they hardly remembered, so she could reunite with Gong-gong. As the two coffins were lowered into the grave, Aunt Xiuying and Mother felt triumphant. Aunt Xiuying's face beamed. She said she was at peace, even though she would never know who had murdered Po-po. The burial, with the symbolic reunion, brought closure to her fifty-year quest.

Fate is fickle in all cultures—one week after Mother returned from Gong-gong's funeral, Uncle Ma was diagnosed with liver cancer. Mother was there for him to the end, as she had been for Father.

Mother was alone again. The neighborhood called her *kefu*, or "husband killer." Though the family rallied around her, her own health suffered during the emotional turmoil, but I was not prepared for the phone call from my brother-in-law saying I had to come home. I was living in Chicago and had just started my first job. It was a week before the Lunar New Year. He said Mother had an allergic reaction to some medicine she had taken for a cold and had suffered massive internal bleeding. I cursed my misfortune and managed to find a flight, arriving at the hospital, dragging my suitcase behind me. Mother seemed surprised. She was quite lucid and in relatively good spirits despite her surroundings. Her cheeks looked sunken and her former radiance was gone. She sat up and hugged me. I talked to her doctor, who said that while they had the bleeding under control, the prognosis wasn't good; his diagnosis was late-stage liver cancer, the same cancer that had killed her second husband. She didn't look like she was dying and I had her transferred to a bigger teaching hospital for a second opinion. "I'm ready to go. I'm going to fight this cancer," she told me. "When I get out of the hospital, I will start all over." I teased her. "If you find another husband, make sure he goes through a medical exam first so he doesn't die on you too fast." Mother was unaware that her relatives had started preparing her *shou-yi*, which was somewhat premature because the cancer was operable and she made a complete recovery. When I phoned a year later, my younger sister told me, "Mother is gone."

"What? When did she die?" I felt faint, my fingers went icy cold.

"No! No! She's married again and has moved into her new husband's house on Western Street," my sister said, and we laughed, nervously at first, at my misunderstanding. According to my sister, Mother and several widows in the neighborhood had registered for a new seniors' dating service set up by the government, which was concerned that, with the disappearance of big families in China, many widows and widowers were living alone without proper care. A nationwide campaign was launched to encourage old people to start a new family and, as a member of the street committee and having remarried, Mother took the lead, which is how she came to meet Uncle Shen, a retired accountant from Shanghai ten years' her senior.

At Qingming, Mother and my siblings carefully maintained the graves of Father and Grandma. For the tenth year of Grandma's death, Mother burned a wardrobe of colorful paper clothing, television sets, a car, and a refrigerator—an expensive offering. Mother always seemed to trip and fall now when she visited the cemetery, scratching her elbows or legs. "That old lady," Mother said. "She hated me when she was alive and she still won't forgive me now that she's in the other world." My younger sister said privately, "Grandma is probably cursing her for remarrying so fast."

Mother visited me twice in the United States, telling my siblings that she wanted to reconnect with me emotionally. Growing up, I had never heard Mother say how much she missed me or loved me. Age had softened her. One day, I came back from a three-day trip and found her waiting for me at the door, just like Grandma did when I was little. When I asked how she was, she replied, "The food had no taste without your being here." I cringed at her endearing remarks but, little by little, I came to accept her love. Time had also allowed me to become more detached from my feelings for Grandma and I could be more objective and understanding of Mother. We grew closer, and as an expression of love, she cooked, serving up her delicious dumplings and winning the adoration of my American friends. Upon her return to China, I called her weekly, giving her updates on my life and hearing her latest gossip about our old neighbors and occasional complaints about my siblings.

In 2005, Mother was alone for the third time in her life. Uncle Shen was hospitalized with Parkinson's disease and when his children finally showed up, it was to squeeze money out of him and insult Mother in front of the other patients. Disappointed by their greed, and by her husband's silence when they insulted her, Mother filed for divorce although she still had strong feelings for him.

I'd been thinking about applying for a green card for Mother so she could come live with me in Chicago. Didn't Father say filial piety attracted good luck? Mother declined—she had heard about how expensive it was to see a doctor in the United States. "I don't want to be a burden," she said. I suggested she live with my brother, who had just divorced, but she brushed that aside too. "I want your brother to find a wife soon."

When we met in Shanghai in September, she told me she was seeing Father and Grandma in her dreams; they were moving into a new building without stairs on a small hill. A month later, she said, sounding nervous: "Do you remember my dream? We received notice from the village that the cemetery is being moved." A university in Xi'an had bought the land and planned to build a new campus. The city was expanding fast and the dead must make way for the living. Father said that disturbing the dead invited untold disaster. Even the Red Guards trod cautiously around ancestral tombs. But the village was offered a lot of money and traditions were no obstacle to progress in the new China. "It was only a matter of time," Mother said. She said a new site had already been found, on a hill farther down the highway. In November, she had my siblings refurbish the gravestones before the winter snows and gifted everyone who was involved in the project with her homemade dumplings. "Now I can relax," she said.

My younger sister called soon after: "Mother has had a stroke." She had fallen from her bed and, unable to move, had lain on the cold floor for two days before a neighbor found her. When we spoke on the phone, she sounded lucid and said she'd lost the use of her right side but was otherwise okay. She asked me to come earlier than I'd planned.

She was in intensive care by the time I got there. She could no longer see or speak. Her kidneys were failing and the doctor said that Mother could die soon without dialysis. I whispered in her ear and asked if she wanted to go through the dialysis. She shook her head and tightened her grip on my hand, tears streaming from her eyes. Seeing that she was giving up, I said, "Ma, let go now. Don't worry about my siblings. I'll take care of them. Just let go."

In the next two weeks, Mother's kidneys unexpectedly recovered. "Your mother is excited about your arrival and her body responds to it," the doctor said. But the recovery was brief. She fell into a coma. I began to be tortured by what I had previously whispered in her ear. Did I say the right thing? Would her recovery have lasted if I had encouraged her to fight for her life?

Night after night, I stayed at her bedside, hoping I could undo what I had said and bring her back to life. My sister even visited Father's grave, praying that he could persuade her to delay her arrival in the other world. A month passed and her condition neither improved nor deteriorated.

When I was back in the United States, my regret over what I had said to Mother was compounded by the image of her lying on the floor after her stroke, helpless and alone. I used to be shocked by the stories about the bodies of seniors in America found rotting in their own homes weeks after their deaths, unnoticed until the smell became too inconvenient to ignore. In China, we heard such stories in school, which were used as examples of how alienated people were in the West from family and friends, how selfish and uncaring these so-called modern societies were. "It is different in China. Children are our protection in old age," my parents' generation used to say. It was hard to believe that the same story happened in my own family.

For several weeks, before calling the hospital I would dial Mother's home phone every day, letting it ring and ring, wishing that she would pick up and that all that had happened would be merely a dream. There were no miracles. The stroke was an irreversible truth. I would call my brother and he would hold the cell phone next to Mother's ear. I played Buddhist music, read books, and told her stories, hoping she could hear.

One day in December, I woke from a vivid dream. Mother had sat up in her bed, hugged me, and uttered three sentences: "I've paid all your debts"; "You've done enough for me"; and "I don't live far away from you." I flew home again for the second time. My plane landed in Xi'an on Christmas Eve. My car got caught in the downtown crowds; teenagers clogged the streets, dressed up in colorful costumes and holding balloons. When had Christmas become a big holiday in China? It felt more like a Halloween night in the United States. The festive atmosphere stopped at the hospital gate. The patient ward, next to the hospital morgue, was eerily quiet. Mother lay in her bed, a grin on her face. Thinking she was happy to see me, I stepped forward to hold her hands and noticed that the grin was frozen. Occasionally she would yawn or open her eyes for a few seconds, but with no sense of her surroundings.

Every dawn, loud spooky sounds of firecrackers and howling pierced the cold morning air. "Relatives are coming to the morgue to get the deceased for cremation," said my brother. "They are lighting the firecrackers to send off the spirit." Even if the soul departed the body only just before cremation, I knew for sure that Mother's soul had left long ago even though she was still breathing.

I wanted to end what I considered to be Mother's suffering. Many Chinese doctors got huge commissions from pharmaceutical companies for prescribing all sorts of expensive medicine to keep patients alive. I recommended terminating all of Mother's treatment. My decision met strong opposition from my brother and younger sister, whom I suspect felt guilty for not keeping a closer watch on Mother and letting her live alone. They wouldn't let her go. When I insisted, they said I was brainwashed by western thinking. "You are becoming heartless, like those Americans. They put their parents in nursing homes. They talk about unplugging life support when old people are still breathing. This is China and you can't get away with it." In addition, they attributed my "inhuman" decision about Mother to the lingering influence of Grandma.

Mother's relatives came to my support and my siblings backed down. On the afternoon of December 31, the doctor stopped medication and Mother died, surrounded by as many relatives as my sister could muster. "Mother would like a big send-off," my sister said, and we made sure the wake was a grand event with an orchestra to play her favorite Henan operas. This cost my brother half a month's salary, which was ironic, as he had probably never bought her a ticket to an opera when she was alive. As Father liked to say, "You can be cheap with the living, but spare no expense for the dead."

At Father's wake seventeen years earlier, I had disliked funeral costumes and rituals. When it was time to mourn Mother's passing, I found comfort in the traditional rituals, and I put on full mourning garb, burned fake paper money, roamed the neighborhood calling her soul back, and smashed a pottery urn to pray for her reincarnation. I willingly took the podium at her funeral, sharing memories and lauding her role in my upbringing. I told stories of how in the 1970s she traveled to faraway places after work to comb the harvested fields for leftover corn to supplement our food ration and how she stayed by Father's hospital bed daily throughout his illness. Many people shed tears during my speech, and I think Mother's vanity was satisfied.

One of Mother's friends suggested that we take her ashes to Henan and bury her with Gong-gong and Po-po. "A woman who married many times should be buried with her parents," she said. "If she is left alone in the next world, all her previous husbands will fight over her."

Fortunately, when Mother was alive, my younger sister discussed the issue of burial with her and Mother had made it clear that she wanted to join Father in his grave. "I think she wanted to remain part of the Huang family," my sister said. On the third anniversary of her death—in 2008—Mother's urn was buried on the hillside next to Father and Grandma. Now that they did not have the coffin to bicker over, I hoped Grandma and Mother would overcome their past differences and live peacefully together.

19.

INEVITABILITY

Father made me Grandma's coffin keeper when I was ten, imbuing the spooky black wooden box with a mythic significance that I could barely grasp. His stories lulled me into believing that Grandma's coffin and our dedication to Grandma's burial would bring blessings and protection for the Huang family. Up until Father's own death, the coffin loomed large in our house and planning for Grandma's burial consumed our lives. In fact, Grandma's coffin was such a powerful presence in my life that it became what may be the most important thing that has shaped my character.

In a big city where the ban on burial was strictly enforced, growing up with a coffin in the house did not give our family the peace and security that Father had promised. We constantly worried about Father's and our own political futures. In school, where we were taught to stamp out old traditions and customs that impeded the Revolution, the coffin stood as an embarrassing reminder of Grandma's old-fashioned ways. We seldom invited friends home and like Father, we learned to separate our public and personal lives.

Father claimed that the coffin and the burial would restore harmony to the Huang family, but instead the wooden box became a constant source of friction and woeful contention among the adults, unwittingly drawing us children into the arguments. Because I always took Grandma's side, I felt estranged for years from Mother and my two younger siblings who were raised by Mother. Today, the division is still palpable among my siblings, flaring up occasionally when we talk about Mother and Grandma.

Following Father's death in 1988, the mere thought of the coffin triggered sadness and resentment in me. I saw the coffin as a curse that led to Father's untimely end. I felt angry at the absurdity and futility of Father's efforts, which deprived my siblings and me of many of the pleasures and opportunities of childhood. Even now, my younger brother still resents Father's neglect as a child. If Father had spent more time coaching him, he said that he would have been admitted to a better senior high school and entered college. His life would have been different from the one he is leading now—managing Father's former company.

During my twenties, I dreaded going home, which was loaded with memories of Father and Grandma. I distanced myself from Mother, who, I was afraid, might swallow me in the same way that killed Father. I yearned to live in a faraway place so I could be free and alone. With $60 in my wallet, the maximum amount that I was allowed to convert from Chinese currency, I landed in the United States in February 1990.

Coming to America enabled me to reinvent myself, living the way I wanted, without the complications of my family. I put myself through graduate school by waiting on tables at a Chinese restaurant and tending lab rats at my university. Like thousands of Chinese students who come to pursue advanced degrees in the United States, I stayed on after graduation, working first as a reporter and then as a public-relations executive. Unlike Father, a die-hard Communist who railed against the land-owning class and embraced the ideal of establishing a classless Communist society, I turned myself into a bona fide capitalist. All the Communist propaganda intended to indoctrinate me seemed to have the opposite effect. Instead of fighting to "liberate the masses from the yokes of capitalism," I work diligently to make money, enjoying a level of material comfort far beyond Father's wildest dreams. The frugal gene that I had inherited from Father has enabled me to buy my first house and then acquire more properties, just as my great-grandfather had done more than a century ago.

Throughout his life, Father trod carefully to shield himself and his family from political turmoil, and he always advised me to stay away from politics. After obtaining my master's degree in public-affairs journalism, I interned with the Illinois General Assembly, where I gained insights into the ways that democracy works in the United States and developed a deep appreciation for political freedom. Little by little, I've overcome my political inhibitions. In my newspaper commentaries, I express my strong support for democratic reforms and human rights in China, especially after my short-term assignment in the mid-1990s with the *New York Times* in Beijing, where I witnessed the government's severe suppression of political dissent.

In the first five years after my arrival in the United States, I sought to cut ties with my past, limiting my contact with family and friends in China. Striving to be an authentic American, I shunned my favorite tofu and noodles and learned to like spaghetti. I tried to imitate National Public Radio announcers in a quest to rid myself of my Chinese accent. I avoided Chinatown as well as the company of other Chinese immigrants. I did such a good job staying out of touch with my culture that I even began to dream in English. While I was on a job in Tibet, I attracted the attention of the local police; my spoken Chinese was so out-of-date that they called me a "full-fledged foreign lackey" during an interrogation.

In the 1990s, I fell in love with a young woman of Jewish and Dutch descent. I moved in with her, believing that I could start a real American family, free from the shadows of Grandma's coffin as well as interferences from Mother and other relatives. To my surprise, Mother never objected to the relationship, especially after she had heard that American women do not demand a large sum of money from the families of their partners at the time of engagement or marriage. Mother simply asked, "Does she like Chinese food? Does she speak our language?" When I answered no to both of her questions, she paused and then said, "When you have kids, I won't be able to take care of them for you." I pretended to be disappointed, but deep down I was relieved. Father had endured the constant sniping of both his mother and his wife all his life. I vowed to never let that happen to me. Unfortunately, the relationship with my girlfriend ended after two years, right before Mother was ready to send a pair of her old earrings to welcome her into our family.

For a while I seemed to have succeeded in not being Father and in carving out a life that bore no resemblance to his. My past became a distant memory.

However, the past has proved to be as difficult to lose as my Chinese accent. A Russian-born professor told me that he had managed to lose most of his accent when he was young, but as he got older it began creeping back. For me, the suppressed memories of my past are not so much creeping back as goose-stepping in great columns to rival National Day on Tiananmen Square, especially after Mother's death in 2005. I find myself being hit by memories of my parents, sometimes with such intensity that I have to stop what I'm doing and let them play out in my mind. I sometimes wake up from vivid dreams of conversations with them, as if they were alive. Sadness and guilt envelop me.

Time has given me new insights into the absurdities of human circumstances. This recognition has allowed me to reevaluate the past family conflicts over Grandma's coffin with the mellowness that comes with middle age. My harsh feelings toward Father's obsession have gradually softened and I have started to understand him more. I now see the coffin, which embodied his devotion to Grandma, as a cohesive force, binding the whole family together in the Mao era, giving us a common purpose, hope, and the comfort we sorely needed. A traditional burial for Grandma was something tangible we could do to express our gratitude to Grandma for sacrificing her life for the Huang family. Most important, Grandma's burial enabled Father to preserve a link with the past even as the Party sought to erase it.

I have also come to terms with the limitations and futility of my attempts to do everything that would make me different from Father. I am becoming more and more like him. On visits to Xi'an, neighbors and friends will comment on how much I have started to resemble Father. I am told I even walk, and sound, like him. In the mirror, I catch glimpses of genetic inevitability—the nose, the lines on my face, and the look in my eyes. When deciding on life's many choices, I have started to detect his invisible hand guiding me.

As a young person, I rejected Father's lectures on Confucian values and shunned my responsibilities as the eldest son. But, unconsciously, I have started to follow his teachings. I quote Father constantly in my articles and talks, and have started to cherish my role as a caring brother in the lives of my siblings and their children. I spent days organizing my younger brother's wedding and put my share of pressure on him to have a child.

Meanwhile, following their recent relocation, Grandma, Father, and Mother are now resting peacefully on a hillside, overlooking the city. Every Qingming Festival, my brother and sisters gather in the cemetery, lighting incense sticks and burning fake paper money. Afterward, my elder sister will call me with a report, claiming that she had specifically asked for Grandma's blessing on my behalf. When Grandma and Mother were alive, my sister was notorious for skipping holiday visits. Interestingly enough, she now attends the grave sweeping ceremony faithfully and with gifts too—fruits, cakes, and stacks of paper cut in the shape of women's clothing, which she burns while chanting, "Hope they fit you well and keep you warm." I also visit the tomb each time I go back to Xi'an. In 2008, when we gathered in the cemetery on the twentieth anniversary of Father's passing, I felt that we could finally put Father's saga to rest and move on with our lives.

In July 2009, a Skype message from my brother changed everything. "Please call right away! I have news on Grandpa's grave," wrote my brother. The son of Grandpa's cousin, now a peanut grower, had reported that a private company was buying the cemetery land from Grandpa's native village and a notice had just been distributed announcing that those wishing to recover the remains of the deceased should do so; unclaimed remains would be tossed away. The peanut grower said the village was planning to build a new cemetery and a space would be secured for Grandpa among the other deceased of the Huang family. If we were still interested in bringing Grandma home, there would be a good opportunity to do it when the developer was excavating Grandpa's tomb, and we could bury Grandma and Grandpa together in the new spot.

The news revived my interest and for months I found it hard to get out of my mind. Father had groomed me for years as Grandma's coffin keeper, but I wasn't even home when she died. Maybe moving the grave would give me an opportunity to make up for Grandma. I began to toy with the thought that perhaps with my brother's help we could complete Father's journey by moving the remains of Grandma and my parents next to Grandpa in their native land. In doing so, a relative of mine warned that I needed to prepare three small coffins or urns and organize a reinterment ceremony. As complicated as it was, I was willing to jump through hoops to get it done.

My idea ignited some heated discussions among my siblings, reminding me of the many dinnertime squabbles over Grandma's coffin between my parents. Surprisingly, my elder sister, who grew up under Grandma's care, took Mother's former stance and strongly argued against the move. She said she liked the proximity of Grandma's grave. "Even though they've been dead for years, I still feel they are part of my life and visiting the graves is part of my annual routine." My younger sister, who had grown attached to Father in his later years, took my side. As for my younger brother, he repeated a phrase that he had been saying bitterly over the past four decades: "You are the eldest grandson. My views don't count and I don't care one way or another." However, he did propose that we could probably bring Grandpa's bones to Xi'an, but the peanut grower ruled against it. "It is always the practice for the woman to join the man, not the other way around."

With the fate of Grandpa's grave pending, I often called home to discuss the best course of action with my siblings. Sometimes, the arguments became so intense that we shouted at each other on Skype and then hung up, vowing never to talk to each other again. Then, with new information coming from Henan, we restarted our discussion. Between the arguments, threats, and cajoling, there was lots of reminiscing about our childhood days. My sisters filled me in with more anecdotes about Grandma and our parents from those years when I was away at school. In a strange way, I was back with my family again. The arguments brought us closer. In addition, revisiting the circumstances leading to Grandma's coffin enabled me to reconnect with our family's past.

In January of 2010, I decided to visit Father's native village in Henan and see for myself the alleged location of Grandpa's grave.

I reached Henan on a snowy November morning. The road was icy, with the bare branches of poplar trees standing lonely in what would be fields full of crops in a few months. The Yellow River, China's second-longest river, resembled dark chocolate with white frosting—brownish water flowing without a ripple between high banks blanketed with crusty snow. Come the melt, the river would turn wild, capable of swallowing hundreds of villages as it had in the 1940s.

It was pitch dark by the time we arrived at the home of Grandpa's cousin. The whole family had turned out. The cousin had a high, oval-shaped face and melancholy eyes that made me think of Father. I felt the strong urge to reach out to him, as if holding his hands would connect me to Father in the netherworld. A stroke had slurred his speech and he frequently choked up with tears as we talked about the years of correspondence between him and Father about Grandma and her coffin. I imagined Father in this very room years ago; the airy, cavernous farmhouse still had a dirt floor, a coal-burning stove in the middle of the room, sacks of what seemed to be wheat piled up in one corner, a few pieces of old furniture shrouded with dust, and a toilet hole in the ground outside in a far corner of the courtyard. The stage was the same; most of the original cast in this drama was dead; but the curtain had yet to come down.

The cousin held in his trembling hands a piece of paper, which he gave to me. "Directions to your Grandpa's grave," he said. "We've been guarding it for years for your father; no one's family cemetery is secure now. They've already converted our family cemetery into farmland and who knows what's going to happen next."

The map marked the gravesite with precise coordinates. I had always harbored suspicions that Grandpa's two cousins were taking advantage of Father and there was no grave. A map wasn't hard proof, but I was relieved enough to think that it all might be true. Over cups of hot, locally grown chrysanthemum tea, we passed the night talking about the past glories of the Huang family. The cousin in his younger days must have been as good a storyteller as Father, which to me made his stroke seem all the more cruel. He told me that my great-great-grandfather was a warrior and an educated military officer in the imperial court. He was a sharp crossbow shooter, like William Tell, and could shoot through a poplar leaf from a hundred feet away. He was credited in the 1860s for capturing the leader of the "long-haired rebels," the Taiping Heavenly Kingdom movement, who fought the Qing Dynasty. This great-great-grandfather acquired several hundred acres of prime farmland along the Yellow River, hiring more than twenty tenants, and the Huang family fortune continued to expand for years after the death of my great-great-grandfather. By the time Grandpa and Grandma were married, this part of the region was called the Huang Estate.

The night was chilly and quiet. As I bundled up in a dusty quilt to sleep, I felt like running a black-and-white movie through my mind. I thought of the stories Grandma and Father had shared with me—the TB epidemic that killed nearly all of the male members of the Huang clan, the flood that stranded them on a tree for three days, the arranged marriage between my eleven-year-old Father and a sixteen-year-old girl, and the big white horses that had been snatched away by the invading Japanese. I stared at the high ceiling, saddened by the tribulations of the Huang family but excited to be "home."

The village looked prosperous in the morning sun. Most families had built big red-brick houses. Peanuts and herbs did well in the sandy soil and incomes were good. Over the years, the village had been moved several times due to flooding, but the Huang cemetery was apparently still where it had always been, outside Chenjiagou Village, home to Chen-style tai chi, and proud of it.

Grandpa's tomb lay across the street from the China Tai Chi Museum. "Many people here have heard about your father's work to preserve your grandpa's tomb," the peanut grower bragged. "Under Chairman Mao, several of our relatives here fought hard to keep the grave marker when the village converted it into farmland. We all waited for your grandma to come back and join her husband, but your father never brought her home." He seemed disappointed that Father had failed to keep his promise;

death was apparently not an acceptable excuse for not honoring a family commitment.

The peanut grower unfolded the map and, using an electricity pole as his reference point, took forty-two steps to his right, and twenty-five steps forward. "This should be it," he shouted.

Having heard about the gravesite all my life, I didn't know what to think at that moment. I hoped Father's spirit was watching. I joined the peanut grower in the snow and looked around us. "Wasn't it supposed to be located on the back of a dragon near the Yellow River? I don't see any water." The peanut grower laughed: "Yes, a branch of the Yellow River used to meander around the village and the legendary dragon resided there, but the Yellow River has changed direction many times over the years and is now to the south." That made sense, and I thought the open view auspicious enough.

We dug a hole in the snow, lit the fake paper money the peanut grower had purchased in the village. I knelt, kowtowed three times to my long-dead grandpa, whose presence I had known all through my life. It felt deeply comforting.

Back in Chicago, I waited anxiously for news from Henan while pondering a permanent solution for Grandma's remains. Then, on a business trip to Henan six months later, my younger brother stopped by Grandpa's tomb to pay tribute. What he encountered was nothing like what he had expected from the pictures I had sent them—the idyllic cemetery and its surrounding farmland had been cordoned off by barbed wire. A construction crew was pouring concrete into the foundation for a new traditional-style building, which locals said would be a tai chi center for foreign and Chinese tourists who trek to the village in search of authentic tai chi training.

According to the peanut grower, whom my brother called to find out the situation, the private developer had convinced the villagers that the building foundation would not go deep enough to disturb the remains of Grandpa and other deceased relatives. "We decided that it is better to leave the remains, rather than moving them since it is bad luck to move the remains of our ancestors around." What the peanut grower did not mention was that he had accepted a sum of money on condition that our family would rescind the rights to excavate and relocate the remains.

As upset as I was that I couldn't protect Grandpa's grave from development, I took comfort in the fact that Grandpa, a practitioner of tai chi, would be part of a building that promotes this ancient form of Chinese martial arts, which Father had hoped that I would continue with. But what about the reunion? An elderly relative, who never failed to come up with solutions for every occasion, made a proposal that my sisters said was the next best thing to physically relocating Grandma's remains. According to the relative, I should gather a cup of dirt from Grandma's grave and buy a wooden dummy with Grandpa's name engraved on it. "Bury the cup of dirt and the dummy next to your Grandma, hold a spirit-calling ceremony, and your grandparents will be reunited," she instructed. When I paused in hesitation, she said, "It will work if you have faith in it."

According to the Chinese lunar calendar, October 1 is Ghost Day—the living bring "clothes" to the dead to prepare them for the upcoming winter. I flew home to observe the occasion.

We brought an urn containing the cup of dirt and a wooden dummy bearing Grandpa's name and placed it next to Grandma's remains. A shaman that my little brother invited from a nearby village presided over the ceremony. Chanting to invoke the spirits of my grandparents, who were supposed to reunite after a century of separation, he lit the incense sticks and set fire to the piles of fake paper money and paper clothes that my sister had purchased. As a plume of smoke rose to the sky, my siblings and I knelt around the grave and chanted along with the shaman, who called upon my grandparents to bring peace and prosperity to the Huang family. Despite the somber atmosphere, I found it incredibly romantic and could not help quoting from Shakespeare: "He is the half part of a blessed man, / Left to be finished by such as she; / And she a fair divided excellence, / Whose fullness of perfection lies in him."

AFTERWORD

Our hometown, Xi'an, was just one vote short of becoming the capital city of China," my late father used to tell me, referring to the period after the Communist takeover in 1949, when a political advisory body consisting of delegates from all walks of life decided on Communist China's capital city. "Otherwise, we could have seen Chairman Mao easily. The government would have built nice buildings like you see in Beijing and people from all over the country would have come to visit us," he continued, smacking his lips in regret.

Growing up in the 1970s, I constantly heard similar sayings from people who believed Xi'an was not chosen as the capital city because of the lack of a Forbidden City. "Only one vote," they would say with a sigh. I searched for evidence and found nothing to support the assertion. Since Xi'an had been the capital city for twelve dynasties, it was not surprising why Xi'an natives would feel that way.

It was true that Xi'an does not have a grand Forbidden City, home to the emperors and their many concubines and eunuchs, but we have plenty of mausoleums and tombs guarded by thousands of terra-cotta soldiers. Of China's two hundred and thirty-one emperors and one ruling empress, seventy-nine of them were buried in and around Xi'an. Emperors would begin scouting for propitious locations for their burial as soon as they assumed power, and work would begin almost immediately on their tombs, the interiors of which resembled a palace so they could enjoy the same glory and luxury in their afterlives. Empress Wu Zetian of the Tang Dynasty spent twenty-three years building her tomb and legend has it that her accession was because of the location of her husband's tomb, nestled between two hills that resembled a woman's breasts and hence a powerful source of female energy.

In March 1975, while digging a well, some farmers outside Xi'an found what looked like pieces of a large statue. They reported what they had found, and further investigation revealed the buried army of terra-cotta warriors and the tomb of Qin Shihuang, the first emperor of a unified China. In that year, Father, a big fan of ancient Chinese history, took me on company-organized trips to see the recent discovery that is now part of the world's cultural heritage. He said the emperor started building his tomb at the age of thirteen. More than seven hundred thousand workers labored thirty-eight years to build it. Historians believe the tomb of Shi Huang, which has been left sealed, was an exact replica of his palace and contains a treasure of unimaginable value. Many of the key builders and craftsmen were buried alive inside the tomb to protect its secret passageways from grave robbers. I had nightmares for weeks.

Chairman Mao admired the first emperor's unconquerable ambitions and his feat of uniting China and heartily commended his brutal crackdown on dissent when Qin Shihuang burned books and buried Confucian scholars alive. As a result, archeologists were allowed to excavate and protect his tomb in Xi'an. In addition, the leadership in Xi'an, known for their conservative sensibilities that were typical of northwesterners, managed to preserve the city wall and a Ming Dynasty bell tower that stood in the middle of the city. Father said the Ming tower with flying eaves was built to conquer a dragon that lay dormant underneath Xi'an and would occasionally wake up to cause earthquakes. Other ancient relics were not so lucky. In their zealous efforts to purge the ancient city of old traditions and customs to make way for the new Communist society, the Red Guards blew up many ancient buildings, smashing and burning whatever was deemed to be representative of China's oppressive and exploited past. In a city as old as Xi'an, there was much to destroy.

With the death of Mao and the ensuing economic reforms, Xi'an, with its ancient history, has now become a cash cow for tourism, with its terra-cotta warriors outside the first emperor's tomb a powerful draw in the global tourism game. The city experienced a rebirth—there is a rush to "restore the past," which could erase forever what is left of the city's history. The last time I wandered Xi'an's "restored" streets, I half expected to see Mickey Mouse in mandarin robes. The courtyard houses were gone. Modern concrete structures punctuated the skyline, and gaudy traditional-style retail outlets lined the widened streets, and loud billboards glittered with the universally exclusive consumerist icons of Chanel and Rolex in the hastening dusk. Where were the giant Chairman Mao portraits and red flags with golden hammers and sickles that were so omnipresent in my youth? They had been replaced by Colonel Sanders and the red-and-gold arches of McDonald's. Still, the children looked happy enough, oblivious to the thousands upon thousands of ancestral spirits drifting homeless around them.

The Hui district of Xi'an's Muslim population retains some of its ancient charm. The narrow streets, towered over by old houses with flying eaves, brought back intimate feelings of our old city. History is empowering. Hundreds of specialty foods in dazzling colors were on display. Amid the hustle and bustle of visitors, the cacophony of cooking and the food vendors' hawking was soothing to the ear. The Hui have managed to remain united and defiant in the defense of their religion and cultural heritage. The government leaves them alone for fear of triggering large-scale demonstrations, which is probably why the district has survived China's modernization unscathed.

The neighborhood where my parents raised me and my three siblings is not so lucky. "You won't recognize it," my brother told me as we left Xi'an's international airport in November 2009. He had sent me an e-mail earlier, reporting that a private developer, contracted by the government, wanted to demolish our old house, ownership of which had passed to me. The house had so many memories that I felt compelled to return home before it disappeared.

Like thousands of former state-owned enterprises, Father's old company had collapsed and its land was being redeveloped as another shopping mall, hopefully not on the scale of the world's biggest mall, which is in Beijing. The warehouses, factories, and administrative buildings had been blasted to rubble, though a handful of stubborn concrete-and-steel support columns had survived. It reminded me of old newsreel footage of the German cities devastated by British bombing toward the end of World War II. Wild grasses were already reclaiming the soil.

We arrived in time for what my brother said was a frequent scene; a crowd had gathered near the entrance of the residential complex, former neighbors barring entry to the demolition teams. The local government wanted the land for a replica Han Dynasty palace, something to do with tourism and restoring tradition. I was unaware of any such link with China's imperial past. The only thing notable about our area was that it was near an execution ground where thugs and counterrevolutionaries were shot dead with a single bullet to the back of the head. Those "thugs" now seemed to have found employment with the government as they did battle with defiant local residents. The government promised that modern and spacious apartments would be built in the distant west of the city. A loudspeaker truck declared that residents had been given ample warning. But they had read and heard about other forced relocations and the empty promises that robbed others of their homes. The old ladies of the neighbor-hood had marshaled themselves as a human wall to block any attempts at forced entry.

My brother said the developer had earlier that morning sent in dozens of men armed with long wooden batons who managed to breach the "human wall," bringing down the gate and smash-ing several windows and a few skulls before being driven back. I saw many familiar faces among the defenders; my former class-mates, the former workshop director, and the friends of Moth-er's, whom she used to dance with every morning in the park. I pulled down my baseball cap, hoping people wouldn't recognize me, but I was spotted by a woman, an old colleague of Father's, who, eyes welling with tears, launched into a tirade: "The gov-ernment is rotten to the core. The leaders are greedy and ruth-less. They've sold the people's property to private developers. They want to make us homeless so neither the living nor the dead can find peace." Would the demolition have radicalized my par-ents, who clung to the past as a source of great comfort? Father might be too orthodox, but I was sure that Mother would have been among the women linking arms and braving the batons.

"I have kept a few items from the house," my brother said. He had sold everything else. "The old stuff is useless. We need to move forward." In China now, people are eager to "move for-ward." Dwelling on the past is "reactionary."

At my brother's house, I realized that he had gotten rid of most of my parents' furniture—our prized antique armoire that Father had bought as "fruits of the Cultural Revolution" was sold to a recycling center because my sister-in-law preferred a new

European-style wardrobe. I held back my anger and sifted through the things he had saved. There was a package neatly wrapped in red cloth. Inside were blue strips of cotton and fabric, which Mother had torn off from Grandma's shirt following her funeral to stuff into our own bedding so some of Grandma's longevity might rub off on us. There was Father's old 1970s Shanghai-brand watch, a major household item that had cost him two months' salary; he had shown off that watch at a "speak-bitterness" meeting at our school to illustrate how prosperous we have become under Communism. There was even one of my old journals, the one with the red cover given to Father by his company on June 18, 1980, when I was in senior high. On the first page, three lines of neatly written characters read: FOR COMRADE HUANG ZHIYOU, A MODEL PARTY MEMBER. Father had given it to me and, like a good Communist, I had filled its pages with inspiring quotes. "A person's life is finite, but the Communist cause in infinite." "When the person merges his life with Communism, making it a whole organic entity, his life will be prolonged and elevated in this common collective cause."

Nobody talks about merging their lives with Communism now, even my sister, a veteran Party member. She reminded me that it was the first day of the lunar month, an auspicious day to go visit Famensi, a Buddhist temple said to have one of Sakyamuni's finger bones. "Your prayers are more likely to be answered today," she said. During the Cultural Revolution, an abbot had self-immolated in a desperate attempt to protect the temple from destruction by Red Guards. His heroic act scared the young rebels. Nowadays, the temple is a major tourist hot spot, and the local government hired a Taiwanese architect who designed and built an ultramodern hall nearby for would-be worshippers, who are charged an exorbitant entry fee. There's a long pathway there, and I copied my sister and lit sticks of incense I had bought from a peasant vendor who cornered me at the entrance and kowtowed to a row of freshly painted gold Buddhist statues. Each statue was for different human needs— reproduction ("please grant me a baby boy"), a child's education, career, and business ("please shower me with more money"), and health. Wealthy people too busy to worship could buy an "everlasting candle" to be placed next to the huge Buddha in a cavernous hall so they had his perpetual blessing. The original temple, with its elegant delicate tower, still stands, lonely on a side lane, guarded by the spirit of the immolated abbot.

On the way back from the temple, we passed by a large stretch of land, which used to be cemeteries and farmland. My sister excitedly pointed out the dazzling new changes—a restored Tang palace, where guards dressed in ancient armored uniforms stood expressionless at the door; a new park with an artificial lake with Tang pavilions built in the ancient style; and a palatial restaurant that would serve "authentic" imperial-court food. I wondered aloud how many acres of prime farmland the government had occupied and how many cemeteries had been destroyed or forced to move. My sister said, "A lot."

In the old days, people preserved their ancestral cemeteries at all costs because the cemeteries served as tenuous links to the past, connecting descendants to their roots. Father used to say that the worst curse one could fling at someone was, "I'm going to dig up your ancestral tomb. You'll have nowhere to go after death." Nowadays, all is transition and impermanence. In today's rapidly changing China, both the living and the dead must give way to development. Villages and cities that we claim as our ancestral homes are being transformed beyond recognition, and ancestral cemeteries are being bulldozed. People are no longer tied to their birthplaces, and as they search for better job opportunities, many have migrated to the sprawling cities and to distant parts of the world.

Grandma desired nothing more than to end her life as a transient and return to her ancestral home to stay forever. For me, however, being able to travel farther away than I ever thought I would has brought a different sense of fulfillment. Each time I conclude my overseas travels and see the familiar skyline of Chicago from the plane, I whisper to myself, "I'm home."

ACKNOWLEDGMENTS

This book represents my effort to make up for my foolish reticence at Father's funeral in November 1988. It is also my attempt to rescue an obscure family story that I believe speaks universally to the contradictions that are thrown in our paths as we grow up. More important, researching and writing this book have given me new insights into my relationship with my parents, Wang Guiying and Huang Zhiyou, whose teachings have continued to shape my character.

The Little Red Guard would not have been possible without the help of my relatives, especially my sisters, Huang Wenxia and Huang Wenjing, as well as my brother, Huang Wenjie, my brother-in-law, Wu Zhiyi, my cousins, Geng Jianping and Hu Honglian, and my nieces, Ren Xiaoyu, Wu Fei, Geng Mingsha, and Geng Mingfei, all of whom have enthusiastically shared with me their memories of our parents. Also in Xi'an, many thanks go to my close friend Liang Li.

In 1988, I met Dr. Robert Crowley, who was a visiting professor in Shanghai. Our short meeting turned into a lifelong friendship. Dr. Crowley reached out to me after the government crackdown on the student pro-democracy movement in 1989 and paved the way for my studies at what was then the Sangamon State University in Springfield, Illinois. Over the years, Dr. Crowley has served as a tireless mentor and advocate, reading and editing almost every article and book that I have written.

I am very fortunate to have Peter Bernstein and his wife, Dr. Amy Bernstein, as my agents. They took me under their wing and assisted me in every possible way with patience and encouragement. I also want to express my gratitude to Philip Gourevitch, who continues to be a champion of my work, and to Esther Allen, whose help has enabled me to embark on my career as a literary translator and writer.

I appreciate the help from Chris Wood and Tim Cribb, who first edited and published an excerpt of the book "Grandma's Longevity Wood" in the *Asia Literary Review*. Tim also provided valuable suggestions and editorial assistance to the first draft. My thanks also go to Christopher Cox and Caitlin Roper, who published an excerpt of the book in *The Paris Review*. In addition, many of John Siciliano's suggestions have also helped shape the book.

I want to thank Patrick Tyler, the former chief at *The New York Times*, Beijing, for those adventurous months we spent in China. That experience changed the focus of my writing.

Chai Guoxing was my dorm mate at Fudan University. Since then, we have never parted. Chai and I ended up in the same school in Springfield, Illinois, and with the same company for several years in Chicago. In the first few years in the United States, he and his wife, aka "cousin" Jane Wang, helped me tremendously, and we spent the most challenging yet happy years together.

In Springfield, Illinois, I was fortunate to have the friendship and help from my professors and mentors Mary and Brent Bohlen, the late Bill Miller, Mike Klemens, Richard and Judy Shereikis, Charlene Lambert, aka Granny, and brother Bruce Kinnett. There is no way I can forget Bill Brown for his generosity over the past twenty years. Wish you a good life in Indonesia, Bill.

When I first arrived in Chicago, Ruth Tregay Siegel and the late Robert Siegel took me under their wing and introduced me to the city and to Chicago politics. At their Lincolnwood home, I was introduced to a group of wonderful family and friends, including Ray, Laura, Anita, Susanne, and Esther. The most memorable moment was when I visited Robert Siegel on the night he fell into a coma. As I held his hand and talked to him, he miraculously woke up and engaged in a long talk with me and Ruth before departing this world. Thank you, Mother Ruth.

I have incorporated into my book many of the heated discussions over TCS and Nietzsche with Maria and Warren Tai. I want to thank the following close friends who have become part of my family: Monica Eng, Colin McMahon, Linda Yu (I'm waiting for your book), Tao Zhang (my close friend and fellow Xi'anese who has taken the photograph for the cover), Michael Bradley of the Chicago Archdiocese (thanks for your editorial assistance), Tish Valva in the UK, Jim and Laurie Nayder, Lih and Frank Wang, Xiaoping Chen, Susan Harris, Juju Lien, Cindy Savio, Kate Durham and the lovely Miss A, the talented Hou family, especially Dong Mama (thank you for the noodles), Andrea Dunaif aka my beloved W, David Alexander, Eiko Terao, Mike and Lynne Coyne, Ho Pin, Yunfei Zhang, Ellen Bork (my favorite editor and friend), Sharon Hom and Mi-ling Tsui at HRIC, my talented alumnae, Jun Chen, Yali and Lily Dong, Rong Shi, Chen Xiaoping, Li Yali and her son Hao Yang, Jan and Karen Futa in Hawaii, James and Diane McClaine, Judy and Todd, Amy and Nick, Susan and Jacob, Linda Tran, Carolyn Alessio, my wonderful friend and neighbor Alice Cooperman, Ingrid Magan, Mary Houlihan, Ed Wojcicki, Chancellor Susan Koch at UIS (for inviting me to a memorable commencement in May 2012), my favorite "sister-in-law" Jill Kinnette (so happy for your recovery), Jane Lawicki, Pat Lawlor and Janice Chambers (thanks for encouraging me to write my book back in 2000), Jackson Hsieh (you are a true brother), and Gary Huang (congrats on your Rotary presidency), Jane Hu (thanks for the proofreading), Robin Xu, and, of course, Caren and Dale Thomas. I want to thank Scott and Caroline Simon as well as my beautiful goddaughter, Lina Simon, and her sister, Elise. I'm indebted to Gerhard Dierkes in Germany for his tireless efforts to help me with my books and translations.

Of course, I'm grateful to my editor, Megan Lynch, for publishing this book, for her great editorial insights, and for granting me creative freedom. I'm also lucky to work with two extraordinary publicists, Claire McGinnis and Elizabeth Hohenadel. And thank you, Ali.

Last, I want to thank a group of supportive friends at work— Thaddeus Woosley (publicist extraordinaire), Hans Van Heukelum (thank you for the little red book), Andrew Delaney, Jessica Wojanis, Cara McCall, William Seyfarth aka Jimmy Annex, Kelly Drinkwine, Tory Neff, and George Zsolnay.